The
Fears
Men
Live
By

The
Fears
Men
Live
By

SELMA G. HIRSH

FOREWORD BY HARRY A. OVERSTREET

Harper & Brothers: New York

Bk II

THE FEARS MEN LIVE BY

Copyright, 1955, by Harper & Brothers. ©

Printed in the United States of America

Library of Congress catalog card number : 55-9697

To
Hannah and Will

For
Lisa and Donna

Contents

Foreword

by Harry A. Overstreet

A decade ago the knowledge made available in this book did not exist. New researches were, indeed, just at the point of being made; but they had not yet been made; and most of what is here revealed was still in the limbo of our ignorance.

Today—thanks to the researches—this new knowledge is available. We can now see in perspective the fears, hostilities and prejudices that have darkened our world; and seeing them thus, we can embark upon a new adventure of wisdom.

What the author of this book has done is something for which we should be deeply grateful. She has translated highly technical psychological material into the language of our everyday life, and she has done it with such lucidity that this material can now enter into the climate of our common thinking.

This is of no small moment, for the knowledge revealed by these psychological researches is knowledge that we desperately need here and now. In one sense, the problem of hostility is the central problem of our time. Knowledge of the causes and workings of hostility—and of its possible cure —becomes, therefore, a central kind of knowledge for this age that is at an acute point of anxiety about its future.

We are having today to redefine and extend our mental equipment for good citizenship. It is by no means enough for us to acquire a periodic body of information about candidates and issues and to add this to a sort of general knowledge about the history and structure of our political institutions. Now information about our human selves must become intimately part of our citizen equipment. For what we do with regard to candidates and issues and the judgments we pass upon our institutions will all largely depend upon our deeper emotional judgments about man and his relationships to his fellow man.

In particular, we need to understand ourselves and one another at the point where our private frustrations are mysteriously converted into public dangers.

Walt Whitman once wrote disdainfully of "poems distilled from poems." In this age, however, of scientific accuracy and tabulated scholarship, we can be grateful for certain types of books distilled from books.

The type of literary art represented in the present volume is by no means a diluting and watering down of the books from which it derives. It is rather the art of making accessible to all of us a knowledge that would otherwise be hidden away on scholarly shelves. Since it is the kind of knowledge that cannot properly perform its function if it has lodging in the minds of scholars only, its rendition into the language of everyday life gives it a chance to do its proper job.

I write this foreword in personal gratitude to the author and in the conviction that a great many people will, like myself, read the book with an excitement that becomes a new sense of responsibility.

Introduction

This should be a heartening book. Its purpose is to provide new insights into the oldest and most troublesome problem of mankind, irrational prejudice and uncontrolled hostility. And insight is a first step in management.

The title is accurate. The central thesis of this book is that people are prejudiced because they are afraid. They use their prejudices to conceal their fears.

Such people generally cannot face the truth about themselves; and the truth, like charity, must begin at home. If one cannot accept the truth about oneself, one cannot possibly accept the truth about others.

Because of their fears prejudiced people are apt to be pessimistic. They project upon the world all of their own deeply-lying despair; they view their fellowmen with anger, never with confidence. Therefore they are inflamed by much of what they see.

Because of their fears prejudiced people also tend to magnify the dangers that surround them. Therefore they search for protection, for someone strong and powerful to cope with the boundless evil they envision.

Temperamentally such people are better suited to undermine a democracy than to live in one. Emotionally they cannot absorb its faith, but they can and do live indefinitely on its fears.

This book attempts to describe how the fears of such people came to be; how they thrive; and how they may be prevented from thriving.

This is neither a scholarly nor a scientific book in the usual sense. But as the acknowledgments at the close of this volume suggest, it owes its existence to many works that are, and particularly to the volumes known as *Studies in Prejudice*. The central volume of that series, *The Authoritarian Personality*, provided the foundation for this book.

Although each of those volumes, reflecting many years of painstaking research by social scientists, psychologists and psychiatrists, approached the phenomenon of prejudice from different vantage points, they concur to a remarkable degree in many of their conclusions. The combination of influences and experiences, the early fears and conflicts, the later guilts and frustrations that join to produce a hostile human being, are starkly recorded in all the volumes.

The Fears Men Live By is not a summary of those extensive works. It is frankly an interpretation of them and for this interpretation the author is solely responsible. This book could not have been written, however, without Dr. John Slawson. Psychologist, social scientist, community relations expert, it was he who, as Executive Vice President of the American Jewish Committee, convened a group of distinguished social scientists, psychologists, and educators, a little over a decade ago, to chart an unprecedented program of research into the dynamics of prejudice. It was his vision and resourcefulness that made possible the execution of that research program and its eventual publication as the *Studies in Prejudice*.

The author was fortunate, therefore, in having had the benefit of Dr. Slawson's counsel throughout the preparation of this book. He read it critically, chapter by chapter, from its first to its final draft. Because of his grasp of the theoretical as well as the practical aspects of this subject, because he saw so clearly the *Studies'* relation to immediate and present-day problems, because of his unerring sense of what is important and what is trivial, he rendered the author singular and invaluable assistance.

It would be unwarranted to assume that the explanations offered by the *Studies* or this interpretation of them are all the explanations there are for the existence of prejudice. Myriad influences are constantly at work upon us. There are, therefore, myriad reasons for our behavior. In noting those personality traits that seemed particularly to be associated with prejudice, the scientists did not suggest that *all* people with such traits are prejudiced, or that these characteristics are present in all who are prejudiced. They simply stated that certain relationships were manifest in the histories of the prejudiced individuals they studied, and because these appeared so consistently, they would probably hold true for many other Americans.

Several thousand men and women participated in the investigations reported by the *Studies*. They came from every walk of life and different income brackets. There were teachers, housewives, servicemen, and veterans just released from army duty. There were several hundred university students. There were business executives, union organizers, laborers, and white collar workers. To discern possible relationships between prejudice and mental disturbance, more than a hundred patients from mental institutions were included in the study. To explore possible links between anti-social attitudes of some criminals and specific attitudes of prejudice, over a hundred inmates from San Quentin Prison were also studied. Because of the scientists' special interest in anti-Semitism and anti-Negro prejudice all participants were white, and either Protestant or Catholic.

In their investigations the scientists used all the tools of their respective trades. For the study of *The Authoritarian Personality,* they developed an important three-dimensional method of exploring individual character. Starting out with attitude questionnaires resembling the familiar opinion polls, they followed these with private interviews conducted by trained psychologists. Finally, they used a series of psychological tests in which an individual unwittingly "gives himself away." None of these techniques was new, of course, but here, for the first time, they were used in the service of one another for the study of individual character.

The questionnaires consisted of a set of opinions covering a wide range of subjects. They considered problems relating to minority groups, to political and economic issues, matters of patriotism and even war and peace. All the statements were worded convincingly, but essentially they were a conglomeration of half-truths and undemocratic notions and by one's agreement or disagreement with them one unwittingly revealed a good deal about himself and his own inclinations. Such statements as these, for example, were included in the questionnaires:

—It is only natural and right for each person to think that his family is better than any other.
—The worst danger to real Americanism during the last 50 years has come from foreign ideas and agitators.
—Obedience and respect for authority are the most important virtues children should learn.

—The business man and the manufacturer are much more important to society than the artist and the professor.

—Sex crimes, such as rape and attacks on children, deserve more than mere imprisonment; such criminals ought to be publicly whipped, or worse.

—One trouble with Jewish business men is that they stick together and prevent other people from having a fair chance in competition.

—There may be a few exceptions, but in general Jews are pretty much alike.

—To end prejudice against Jews, the first step is for the Jews to try sincerely to get rid of their harmful and irritating faults.

—It would be a mistake ever to have Negroes for foremen and leaders over whites.

—The people who raise all the talk about putting Negroes on the same level as whites are mostly radical agitators trying to stir up conflicts.

—Most Negroes would become overbearing and disagreeable if not kept in their place.

A "high" score on the questionnaire meant that the individual agreed with most of these statements and a good many more like them. A "low" score meant that he rejected most of them.

The questionnaires were for the purpose of discovering which attitudes *seemed* to go together. The interviews and tests were then used to see whether they actually *did* go together, and if so, why?

Trained interviewers spent from one to three hours with a selected number of "high" and "low" scoring men and women of various backgrounds and interests. They encouraged them to talk of anything that interested them—politics, jobs, family, friends, their war experiences, their views about love, marriage and children, their thoughts about the future.

All were asked about their childhood. What did they

remember particularly about their parents? What were the outstanding events in their childhood? What were they themselves like as children? They were asked about their achievements as well as their failures—at school, on the job, in marriage, or wherever.

The interviewer listened and observed. Notes were made not only of what was said, but how it was said. Puckered brow, tight lips, shifting eyes, fugitive smiles, diffidence or candor in manner, resentment or warmth or arrogance in speaking—all these contributed to the interviewer's report.

His notations were then turned over to raters who had not seen the persons being interviewed, nor did they know whether their questionnaire scores had been "high" or "low." Systematic summaries of the predominant attitudes, feelings, and experiences of each individual were then prepared and matched with each one's questionnaire results to discover the differences—if any—revealed by the interviews between the "highs" and the "lows."

The scientists realized, however, that information gained during such interviews, no matter how skillfully handled, was not entirely dependable. There is a perfectly human desire to make one's revelations acceptable to the listener, and some willful as well as wishful distortions are almost certain to creep in. There is also the possibility that the interviewer might unwittingly color his interpretations. But most important of all, many people are understandably hesitant about sharing their innermost thoughts with someone who is strange to them.

To probe those innermost thoughts—to make them audible as well as visible—two well-tried psychological tests were used. The first, the *Thematic Apperception Test*, or TAT, perfected almost twenty years ago, is today widely used in all kinds of diagnostic research efforts. This test consists of a series of photographs, each quite different from the other, but each suggesting any number of situations and moods so that the person being tested could see whatever he wished to see in them. A total of one hour was allowed to tell a story about the ten pictures. As in any creative undertaking, it was expected that the story-teller would put "something of himself" into his creations and would reveal a great deal about himself in this way.

In addition to these picture-story tests, eight simple questions were asked, as, for example, What moods do you find most unpleasant? What great people living or dead do you admire most? If you knew you had six months to live and could do anything you pleased, what would you choose to do? What might drive a person nuts?

When all the results were assembled from questionnaire, interview, and special tests, the job of scoring was not a simple arithmetic undertaking or a mere compilation of opinions. It was to discern threads where none may have been noticed before. It was to forge links between attitudes and feelings, events and experiences—for any number of chains that might not have been previously identified.

Some links were immediately evident, as, for example, the connection between recollections of the past and hopes for the future; between views about obedience in children and notions about leadership and good government; between intolerance and pessimism; between prejudice and the capacity—as well as the desire—to love.

Throughout all of the *Studies* the evidence was indisputable: by the sum of their responses, prejudiced individuals proclaimed their boundless fear. Whether banker, student, housewife or laborer, prisoner or mental patient, the prejudiced personality presented a monotonously oppressive self-portrait. They were people struggling incessantly against long odds and "tough breaks," experiencing innumerable defeats—all because of events they could not possibly prevent, or because of people who were out deliberately to do them harm.

Their prejudices were never isolated attitudes. They hated not just one group of people but several groups; not just one kind of person but many kinds of people. In short, their prejudices were simply an extension of their entire philosophy of life. To the prejudiced all the world was a jungle and the people in it little better than beasts.

The *Studies* have been re-examined many times since their initial publication several years ago. Evaluations and extensions of them are still being reported. Although many have assailed their statistics, calling for greater rigor in method, the fundamental relationships asserted in those volumes have yet to be proven invalid. That these relationships should have been spoken of by the sages in every age does not make them less noteworthy. It does not mean that Confucius in his sayings and Solomon in his proverbs were far ahead of their times when they, too, spotted the child that persists in every man; or that Shakespeare was a prophet when he wrote that "the fault . . . is not in our stars but in ourselves. . . ."

Nor does it mean that our present day scientists are far behind *their* times.

What it does mean is that through studies such as these we are in touch with the fundamental truths about human nature that apply to *all* times. As these truths are translated into the idiom of our own age, they may help us in our present ordeal by offering a view of ourselves that is closer to the truth and therefore to freedom in our own time.

S. H.

Part One

The Dimensions of Fear

——————

1

The Prevailing Fever

This is a story about average Americans who for one reason or another have more than an average amount of fear. It is a true story for it is based upon their own confessions. The "confessions," though, were unwitting ones and those who made them would be the last to recognize themselves.

In the turbulent period in which we live fear is an inescapable emotion of all thoughtful people and in their current anxiety Americans have much in common with most of Western civilization. But the fears around which this story is built transcend these times: they pre-date them and they may even outlive them.

Our theme is well stated by one observer of the current American scene. "It is neither God nor the physical universe the American fears," said Francis L. K. Hsu, "since he sees himself as the associate of one and the master of the other. What he truly fears is his fellowman."

It is startling to contemplate that the most impelling fear in our land may be the fear of one another. For our history and our heroes, all our mottoes and creeds, provide solemn testimony that we are a people whose allegiance is to one an-

3

other and to liberty and justice for all. But because such enmity is not a part of our national image, we may be slow to discern it and even slower to admit that Mr. Hsu has compressed into two stark sentences more than a century of our national history and character.

With the help of our historians we might well trace our present apprehensive heartbeats almost to the beginnings of America herself. All the stories of our epic past recall the persistent image of the pioneer advancing by horse or wagon over rich prairies and burning plains, contending bravely and almost always victoriously with his enemies—and in the end settling down to enjoy in peace the land he had won for his children and his children's children.

Pioneer hardships were real, but eventually they yielded to enterprise and thrift. Dangers were great, but the forces of violence ultimately succumbed to the forces of right. Ignorance was widespread, but sooner or later it, too, generally gave way to the forces of enlightenment. Freedom and justice were virtually household words in those pioneer times.

But the post-Civil War story is something else again. For when villages stretched to make cities, when barns were converted to factories, and when shops became office buildings, the alteration was more than architectural. In fact, there are those who maintain that America's industrial revolution reached deep into the national soul and split it wide open.

For then the earlier pursuit of freedom and justice had to be tacked willy-nilly onto the newer pursuit of money and know-how. The founding fathers' gospel of liberty had somehow to be hammered into the newer gospel of workability.

This was the beginning of the war between two most important strains in our national temperament—our idealism and our materialism. This was the time when *strength* came to mean *hardness*, and *goodness* came to be linked with *weakness*. Aspirations were respected only if they were backed by considerable aggression, and artistic and intellectual activities—like the earlier idealism—were looked upon as luxuries for the few who could afford them.

It was also the era of maxims: "A man works best when he works for himself"; "Success is its own reward"; "A man can measure his success by the regrets, the envies, and the hatreds of his competitors." The maxims reflected the changes in the land and its people. Opportunity no longer over-indulged the land; and the people were coming to know that something more than courage, enterprise, and diligence were needed to ensure their prosperity.

In the saga of our country's growth, then, in the evolution of our industrial genius, may be found the beginnings of the conflicts that wrack us and the fears that invade us today. For here are the beginnings of the contradictory commandments now so firmly woven into our culture that we hardly know which, indeed, we are truly to heed. Our public declarations of brotherhood? Or our private ambitions that urge us to surpass our brothers? Back and forth we shuttle between public creed and private need never knowing precisely when to decry, and when to reward, the aggressive amongst us.

Facing our Hypocesy

These contradictions and confusions spurred originally by our country's phenomenal economic growth, today spill over into many aspects of our lives other than economic, and influence profoundly our thoughts about each other.

Some of the more far-reaching effects, for example, are observable on any sunny afternoon on any park bench in any city in the United States. There sit young mothers, each desperately anxious to rear her young one to be tough enough, yet not too tough; to play fair, but not to get pushed around; to be considerate of others but to "look out for himself." Consequently the clashing admonitions she shouts from her perch sound something like this: "Don't stand there—hit him back!" "Leave him alone—he's smaller than you are!" "Stand up to him—or he'll take *all* your toys!" "Don't start anything—I saw you push him!" "He's bigger than you are—keep away."

She is never sure, really, whether what she is saying makes sense. Maybe in this dog-eat-dog world of ours the boy *ought* to be tough. But then, what mother wants to raise her son to be a lout? In the compromises she finally settles upon, she has much in common with her maternal ancestors who were responsible for raising generation after generation of young men able to fight admirably, albeit reluctantly, whenever they had to—whenever someone tried to push them around.

It is possible, some experts of human behavior suggest, that this time-honored image of ourselves as "fighters, yes—but *only* in self-defense," has something to do with our voracious appetite for scapegoating. When one has an irresistible impulse to push, what could be more human and more in accord with our training than to convince oneself first that "*he*, not I, started pushing. I am merely pushing back."

Some observers of our social scene suggest that the study of our peculiar national anxiety is essentially a study of the contrasts so characteristic of America and Americans. There is, to begin with, the striking contrast between the intent and the effect of our heritage: the disparity between the splendor of our principles and the tarnish of so many of our practices; between the loftiness of our aspirations and the mediocrity of so many of our achievements.

There is our American success system, that symbolic ladder up which all but the incompetent or the unworthy are expected to scamper. There is the perpetual climb to mythical heights and the perpetual pursuit of dreams, however unrealistic they may be. Ours is a land of colossal expectations —and the disappointments are in direct proportion.

Moreover, our country's economic health requires that our appetites be whetted increasingly for bigger and better and more things than we presently own or than most can probably afford. For the nation's business and industrial leaders and most of its political leaders are in full agreement that consumption, not production, is now the ruling factor of our economy. Our earliest heroes may have been those who met the challenge of the land and its elements, and our later heroes may have been those who built and controlled our massive industrial machines—but today's heroes will be those who can discover and tempt the consumer.

The nation's psychologists shudder to think of the emotional hazards in an environment where people are urged to become as competitive in their spending as they are in their earning. In such a situation all agree that hen's teeth might be easier to come by than inner serenity and love of one's fellow man. For what we *are* is considered not nearly so important as what we *own*. The things we have acquired are not nearly so important as the things others have acquired and we cannot yet afford. Our progress is judged only in relation to the progress of others—by the number we have surpassed and those we must still outdo.

Naturally, in such an environment, one's occupation is selected for the purchasing power it provides. The satisfactions in life then swiftly become things we have bought and the prestige we have acquired, rather than inner satisfactions, warm feelings, and experiences we enjoy with, or because of, one another.

Where the possibilities *seem* to be limitless, where success is relative and competition intense, fear of one another is fanned incessantly. There is constant temptation to explain one's failures in such a way as to keep one's vanity intact: by blaming them on anyone and anything but oneself. There is also infinite need for security and an infinitesimal chance of attaining it. There is profound loneliness. And there are endless crowds.

For in a crowd one's solitude is made to seem imaginary; one's disappointments are merged with the disappointments of countless others and the hurt diluted thereby. In the crowd there is surcease from the endless strain of striving: one need not be better than those around him—in fact, one dare not.

In recent times particularly, crowd-mindedness has been described as the prevailing fever among Americans. In many of our communities super-conformity has actually become synonymous with good citizenship. Deviation from the prevailing custom and sentiment is likely to be greeted with criticism resembling moral condemnation.

In our present atmosphere once the circle is drawn, though the compass may have been set to the "average person's" dimensions, it becomes increasingly difficult to tamper with its boundaries. There is distrust of those who try to, contempt for those who are not enclosed within the circle,

esentment of those who dare to move beyond it. Before long,
not only are the actions of those who behave "differently"
called into question, but their intentions and perhaps even
their origins—should these too differ from most. Today in
many places and in fleet succession, the popular has become
the typical, the typical has become the customary—and the
customary has become the correct and finally the only acceptable action, intention, or origin.

But if this fear of the different be the prevailing fever, why
is it that although the fever is all around us, only some succumb to it while others appear to be immune? Why, of those
whom it does touch, are some able to throw it off, while
others, once having submitted, become delirious and may
even rave?

A decade ago a group of scientists in the field of human
behavior asked themselves these questions. For even at that
time, when we had barely begun to recover from the effects
of our global battles in defense of human rights, opinion
pollsters were busy taking the nation's pulse and checking
the national temperature on some matters relating to individual freedom in our own land. With varying degrees of
fanfare these surveyors reported that anywhere from 30 to
60 per cent of the population showed some hostility toward
one or more minority groups in America.

But then, as now, there were many who refused to attach
importance to the matter. Then, as now, of the many "never-
mind" opinions that were voiced, most frequent by far were
those that insisted that prejudice is so universal as to be
practically a part of the natures of us all; that fortunately the
American variety of prejudice is for the most part "mild"
and relatively "harmless," therefore nothing need be done

about it. Indeed, since it was so widespread, nothing *could*
be done about it!

But there were some, even then, who did not agree. They
believed that such hostility, far from being a part of human
nature, should be considered a grave distortion of human
nature and a tragic epitome of our fear of one another.
The more widespread such distortions, they declared, the
more they might be expected to impede and endanger our
country's progress.

This coming together of sociologists, psychologists, and
psychiatrists to study the nature of this hostility was a remarkable event. For in our age of specialization it is almost
as difficult to introduce the experts to one another as it is to
introduce them to all the rest of us. This meeting of minds,
moreover, occurred in a field in which the arguments among
the various schools and disciplines not only seem inter-
minable but usually are: Is man responsible for society or
society responsible for man? Are we slaves to our inner
drives or to our environment? Are our grownup feelings at-
tributable to the childhood that haunts us or to the adult pressures that constrain us?

In the design and execution of their studies, these scientists assumed that men and women are the sum of everything
that happens to them in their lifetimes, that each of us is a
blend of history and heredity, of culture and biology, a
bundle of memories and expectations, habits and manners,
impulses and inhibitions. All these and more determine our
behavior, but the ingredients of the mixture are in different
proportions in each of us.

Though the intention was to study prejudice, the plan was
to study personality, since in the same environment all of us

do not behave in the same way, or yield in the same degree to the pressures around us. To sustain irrational prejudice there must be more than an atmosphere conducive to it. There must be individuals who respond to such an atmosphere.

The scientists were interested in investigating the well-springs of these individual responses. Accordingly, they examined not only the *attitudes* of the prejudiced but the crucial events and the critical experiences in their lives. They inquired into the way these people felt about themselves as well as about others, and how they felt about life generally. They probed into their memories, opinions, hopes and fears. In this way they discovered the nature and the molding of the prejudiced personality.

Their findings, until now known only to scholars, throw considerable light on the cause and the course of the prevailing fear-fever.

Their findings are the essence of this book.

2

The Beginnings

> The beginnings of all things are weak and
> tender. We must therefore be clearsighted
> about beginnings, for as in their buddings we
> discern not the danger, so in their full growth
> we perceive not the remedy.
>
> —MONTAIGNE, 1565

In countless ways grownups appear to live their adult lives
in subservience to, sometimes in rebellion against, their
childhood. But rarely do they live independently of it.

Fears experienced at the age of four will often shape the
thoughts and guide the acts of the forty-year-old. Even
visions of the future emerge from memories of the past, so
that what we remember experiencing is more often than not
what we expect to experience again in years to come.

The *Studies* were rich in evidence on this score. Where
the memories were of warmth and affection, satisfactions
and achievements, so, generally, were the expectations.
Where the memories were of paths too steep or of penalties
too severe, the expectations seemed regularly to match the
memories and the outlook appeared dark and fretful.

Revealing too were the descriptions some men and women

gave of themselves as children. For frequently these were masterly renditions of the qualities and traits that disturbed them still. Those who currently paraded a puritanism for which they were hardly suited, loved to relate what hell-raisers they *had* been. Those now painfully frugal were eager to recall what spendthrifts they *were*. Those who today feared the demands of love more than they desired it—how anxious they were to tell of the days of their youth when ardor was unrestrained and they were forever playing the role of Romeo!

But through all the reminiscing of childhood moods and memories, in all the ways they remembered mother, father, sisters, and brothers, in the events that had stirred them, the experiences that had pained them—in all of these, as we might suspect, the stories of the highly prejudiced differed strikingly from the others.

Whenever the prejudiced "remembered Mama" they seemed determined to make her what a "Mom" should be. In their interviews she was cited repeatedly for her self-sacrifice, her devotion, her goodness, and not infrequently for her beauty. Father was recalled as the family provider—either good or bad—and in terms of the iron hand with which he ruled, or failed to rule, his roost. To the question "What were your parents like?" the highly prejudiced usually replied by describing what they *looked like* and what they had given to their children in the way of material comforts and physical care.

To the listener, the parents of the prejudiced were barely distinguishable from one another. If they had possessed distinctive qualities, these apparently had not been observed by the child-now-grown who was describing them. Of if they had been observed, he somehow could not bring himself to speak of them lest he unwittingly appear to be critical. For an adult it is difficult enough to criticize the object of one's veneration; for a child it is impossible. And it was almost as though these adults still lived in their childhood, in the days when they dared not judge the paramount objects of their reverence, the gods and goddesses who were their parents.

Those low in prejudice, by contrast, were immensely personal in their descriptions of their families and earliest years. They more often described the *feelings* of their parents than they did their physical appearance. They were more inclined to remember the love, affection, and understanding in their homes than the comforts they had lacked or possessed. If they stressed some qualities of their parents, these were the unique and not the conventional ones. They liked to tell of their unusual interests, their rare hobbies, their special talents. They seemed little troubled by the possibility that the pictures they were giving of their backgrounds might be quite different from those given by others.

Being neither distressed nor embarrassed by the shortcomings of their parents, they often described these with humor, or with the quick sympathy that is close to the core of love. For the adults low in prejudice had long ago come to realize that all humans are fallible. To recognize and to speak of their parents' imperfections seemed to them to make those parents not less, but much more, human.

The frailties of memory must be reckoned with, of course. Time may be either a compassionate or a dispassionate artist. The mind can recoil from a memory as indeed it can invent one. But *the way things are remembered* is as important as the accuracy of the memory, and there is something to be learned not only about those who truly experienced whatever they recall, but of those who wish to think they had.

It did not really matter, for example, whether the parents of the "highs" or the parents of the "lows" were actually as they had been described. But it mattered a great deal that the highly prejudiced regularly recalled their parents as the providers of things, rather than of love and affection; and that now as adults they too showed an overweening concern for the material in life, and all their present human ties were ties of obligation rather than of love.

Almost without exception, the prejudiced individual asserted that for him the staples in life were the house he owned, the car he drove, the job he held, the neighborhood he lived in, the club he belonged to. Around them he built his entire view of life—making a virtue of the things he had and an evil of those he did not have. But even as he did this, the best he could say for the values he had chosen to glory in was that "these things, at least, have not yet been proved worthless!"

Whether such a person had never known any other of life's pleasures, or whether now he chose to forget them, it was clear that the reason for his philosophy rested in his experience.

Long before Montaigne, whose wise sentences head this chapter, seers were remarking on the importance of beginnings. For centuries it has been known to civilized peoples that love in childhood is an arch to adult love; that if our childhood experiences were never stretched to include it, our adult perception can rarely imagine its dimensions. The habit of loving, the patterns of love, the lessons of love—these must be learned early and rehearsed regularly through the growing years. If they are not, it is likely that we will play all the roles of our later life like callow understudies, and our performances in the realm of love will rarely, if ever, be enduring ones.

In the *Studies,* the prejudiced were the first to admit that from their earliest beginnings they became intimate not with love, but with fear. For oddly enough, although their parents were often "ideal," and frequently "the best one could ask for," the childhood they recalled was never ideal nor even a remote second best. The narratives of their youth were shrill with resentment. If there were sisters or brothers, they, not the narrator, were preferred by the parents—though the narrator was by far the most amiable of them all. At school he was diligent, often keen, but the teacher bullied or ignored him. On the ball field he was incredibly swift, but the coach unreasonably passed him over. Though he knew and admired many nice girls, youths less noble and worthy than he invariably won them.

Their memories were monotonous episodes of terror, despair, and deprivation. Punishments were frequent and, what was worse, threats of them were perpetual. The "rules" that governed his childhood often seemed to the prejudiced patently unfair, frequently incomprehensible. The penalties remembered had more to do with father's availability or mother's mood than with any well-defined principles. Their tales became cheerful only when they recounted the outrageous things they had "gotten away with"; they became almost timorous when they remembered the many minor offenses for which they had been brutally punished. If they remembered rewards, these were usually meagre or unjustly withheld. If they remembered sympathy, they remembered also that all hope of it vanished when wrongs were discovered and penalties imposed.

As the prejudiced often recalled vividly the physical appearance of his parents, so did he recall with astonishing regularity the strength of one and the weakness of the other. The memory of the strong parent, moreover, was hopelessly tangled with the memory of the appalling contrast between that strength and his own childish weakness—the weakness that had required him to surrender repeatedly to rules he could not fathom, to accept punishment he did not deserve, to show respect and admiration when all he could feel was fear and fury.

But even as he remembered these things, the prejudiced would spring to defend them—and generally to explain them. He would recall himself as "an incredible devil," a "weak sister," or "a small savage" who unmercifully plagued his overburdened mother and his overworked father. In fact now that he himself was an adult, he agreed entirely with the philosophy of the strong parent and spoke cautiously, almost apologetically, of the weak one.

In all his tests, and particularly in the tales he dreamed up for the photographs he was asked to describe, his stories were studded with rebellion and revenge against the elderly. Through the eyes of the characters he created it was quickly apparent that to him youth was a time of miserable dependence, with haunting dreams of rebellion and dreadful fears of punishment. Old age, with physical power spent and outward charms withered, was misery: elderly persons in any photograph were described repeatedly as "defeated," "help-less," "whining," "demanding."

Yet, in questionnaire and interview, the prejudiced advo-cated the importance of obedience above all in children. They could hardly imagine anyone baser than one who would not respect and revere his elders!

Since at an early age, "right" had become that which he was able to get away with, and "wrong" that at which he was caught and for which he was punished, as an adult he lacked any inner guides or checks on his own behavior. Even now he governed his actions largely by the reactions of others, being greatly if not entirely influenced by the possibility of gain-ing their approval or suffering their disapproval. For the prejudiced, public opinion seemed by far the most devastat-ing of all tyrants.

Since the memory of childhood weakness was nearly the bitterest memory of all, it was from this the prejudiced seemed particularly determined to flee. In every way he could think of, now that he was adult, he was anxious to align himself with the strong and to demonstrate as often as he could his right to be there. He spoke proudly of his tough-ness and related countless incidents to prove his ruthlessness. He was quick to condemn and eager to punish any and all who, unlike himself, had failed to "outgrow" their weakness.

The endless "must-nots" remembered from his childhood were the must-nots he now imposed upon others. The behavior he now found repellent in others was the behavior for which he had been most severely rebuked long ago. The penalties he now exacted from others were the penalties that had once been exacted from him. And he rendered his verdicts instan-taneously, for to pause for reflection would be to admit the possibility of remembrance of his own acute and early suffering in the wake of similar verdicts. If there was one thing the prejudiced seemed certain of it was this: he must punish others as others had once punished him. Only by unjustly inflicting cruelties upon others now, could he wipe out the malignant memory of cruelties once so unjustly inflicted upon him.

But just as he could not forget his childhood weakness, neither could he seem to overcome it; and even as he fled from all reminders of it he appeared to be searching for someone who might help him. Because he was determined never again to "knuckle under," and also because he could not bear the thought of life without someone to lean upon, he was driven to find a person with monumental strength and inordinate power to whom he could submit. For thereby he was convinced that far from losing face he would gain the prestige and exaltation that come to those in the presence of, or close to the heart of, power.

It was different for those low in prejudice. The tales they told of their early years frequently echoed joy and confidence, warmth and security. Often they too recalled anger over past injustices; but these never seemed to rankle permanently. It did not make them anxious to become the dispensers of future injustices any more than the sorrows they poignantly remembered made them inhospitable to future joys.

In the photographs they were asked to describe, youth was to most a time of eager striving and intricate planning, old age a time of wisdom and serenity. Where young and old were photographed together they were generally described as "talking things over," "working things out," or simply "discussing things of mutual interest." "Independence," in contrast to the oft-repeated tales by the prejudiced of sudden "rebellion," was pictured as a gradual achievement. In the stories told by those low in prejudice, rarely was anyone described as "laying down the law"; no one was smiling and submissive "on the outside" all the while storing up resentment "on the inside."

When those low in prejudice recalled their parents, they were likely to remember not the dominance of one or the submission of the other, but the way they felt about each other and about their children. What they had learned from their parents was not what they were told but what they had observed. Whereas the highly prejudiced seemed to have acquired involuntarily the worst qualities of either or both parents, those low in prejudice often freely admitted that they consciously tried to incorporate into their own behavior the best of each parent.

Since father was generally remembered as "relaxed" and "mild-mannered"—rather than iron-fisted—the low prejudiced adult did not learn, either by precept or example, that "toughness makes the man." As they often recalled creative and esthetic interests in the family, they were reminded of pleasant leisure-time experiences, and relaxation now seemed to them an important aspect of life. Unlike the highly prejudiced, they never related the virtues of work to the evils of idleness, for they often found pleasure in their work, and their leisure time, far from being idleness, was frequently devoted to some absorbing interest or hobby.

Those low in prejudice usually had no difficulty remembering the times when "right" and "wrong" came clearly into focus. They remembered too that when discipline was imposed in their childhood, sympathy was usually not far off. The rules they remembered, moreover, were principles and guides for future action rather than punishments for past acts and deterrents from later ones; and these had applied to people and situations outside as well as inside their homes. Although the reasons for the rules were usually quite clear, the low prejudiced often remembered many occasions on which they were permitted to question them, even to experiment with them. It was in this way that they had learned the variety of situations to which rules might apply—and the possibility of exceptions as well.

Since the authority they had known in their childhood had been reasonable and even comforting, the low prejudiced adults rarely seemed impelled either to defy or worship all the later authorities in their lives. Whether from parents, teacher, boss, or government, they could readily imagine seeking guidance or help. Nor were they likely to consider either the seeking or the acceptance of such help to be shameful or ignoble. If they chastised anyone because of their dependency, which they readily admitted, they would chastise only themselves. To be sure they had many complaints about the world but these were specific rather than general. They seemed to have more to do with principles than with personalities, with present happenings rather than with past resentments.

It might be said of most of those low in prejudice, that their quarrels with the world were in the nature of lovers' quarrels, in which the fundamental attachment they felt was not one whit diminished.

The process of growing up, we are often told, is a process of disentanglement, and then substitutions. We must disentangle ourselves from people and sentiments, and then we must substitute, for the bright fanciful hopes of our youth, the longer, more flexible plans of maturity. When the process does not proceed as it should, or when it fails even to get underway, then we see an adult physically full-grown, but, in the words of an early Greek philosopher, "a child at man's estate, one whom nature huddled up in haste and left his best part unfinished."

This perhaps explains why there are those among us whom we must call the "highly prejudiced," or simply "the prejudiced." For clearly all the events in their lives have conspired to keep them from achieving maturity. They were not taught how to grow but how to submit to those already grown. They were not taught to understand but to obey; not to try but to keep from trying; not to love but to revere. For them there were no gradual disentanglements, no natural substitutions, no new faiths to replace old fears, no new confidence to dislodge the old uncertainties.

Although the prejudiced had learned early to suppress his anger, and though once he could and did bury the reasons for his fear, he could not bury the fear itself. Many years later he lives with it still. Nor is the terror any less terrifying because its origins have been dutifully forgotten; for now that it is nameless, it is also boundless.

Convincing as it might appear, all this evidence has, of course, to be based upon today's reconstruction of yesterday's events. The brick and mortar are but hints and echoes; and hindsight can be imaginative but it is not necessarily precise.

The scientists themselves were among the first to recognize this. Dr. Frenkel-Brunswik, an important contributor to the original *Studies*, particularly in the area of childhood influences, proceeded therefore to further investigations directly with children—1500 of them between the ages of ten and fifteen. Like the adults, the youngsters were first given questionnaires on issues of the day, including some questions relating to minority groups. As in the adult tests, a smaller number were then selected from among the highest and lowest scorers for interviewing and psychological testing. But then one additional step was taken: the investigators went to the homes of a selected number of youngsters to discuss with their parents, privately and at length, their attitudes toward their children, the goals they held for them and for themselves, their views about child-raising, discipline, and family living.

To note their final findings first: it was easily apparent that parents of the prejudiced youngsters relied heavily upon discipline and strictness in the upbringing of their young. They often appeared anxious for reassurance as to the behavior of their offspring—how did they compare with others, and did they reflect the rigid training they were being given? They made it clear that they did not approve of children "running wild," as so often seemed to them to be the case in the homes of those whom they considered very much poorer or very much richer than themselves. Many had hopes that were almost fantasies of bettering their own status. They spoke of the possibility of a surprise inheritance from a rich and sometimes unknown uncle, of sweepstakes winnings, or some wondrous and unexpected event that might give them the chance they felt they never had. They were anxious that their young achieve the success that had passed them by: they liked to think that their children might become "important," "famous," "a good deal richer than we are." Their chances, according to the parents, seemed to be linked entirely to the possibility that "fate might be good to them" or that luck would be on their side.

The parents of the low prejudiced youngsters, on the other hand, seemed more anxious to discuss the personalities than the behavior of their children. They spoke with enthusiasm of their special interests and particular capacities. They talked of the importance of *guidance* for the young rather than *obedience* from them, and placed far greater emphasis upon encouragement than on condemnation in dealing with their offspring. Much more often than the parents of the more prejudiced children, they described their own goals in life in terms of achieving emotionally satisfying relationships, and being in occupations that were pleasurable as well as interesting. They were anxious for their children to take pride in their own accomplishments, to learn that individual effort is essential for achievement. They rarely mentioned "fate" as a factor in their own or their children's destiny unless it was to reject it, for they would often suggest that even in these precarious times there were many things a person could do to improve his lot if he were so determined.

And as we might expect, the children directly reflected their heritage.

In their interviews the youngsters were asked to describe "the perfect father," "the ideal teacher," the "perfect boy," or "perfect girl," and the "best occupations."

The prejudiced youngster often suggested that his own was the perfect father: one who saw that his children were well-clothed, fed, and housed, who gave them money for things they needed and sometimes for extras, one who could "manage his children" or "keep them in line." The ideal teacher was one who was "strict," who could control her class and "see that the kids did everything they were supposed to do." The perfect boy was tough, a "regular fellow" who could fight in the gang for his rights, but who also did what his elders told him to do. The perfect girl was "ladylike," never a "tomboy"; she was sweet, well-mannered, "never filthy-minded or dirty," and stayed out of the boys' way unless they invited her to join them. The best occupations were well-paying, "good clean work," "something important," "positions with real influence, like a judge or public official." The worst jobs were "the dirty jobs": garbage collecting, street-cleaning, and ditch-digging.

The youngsters low in prejudice, on the other hand, considered the perfect father to be someone who was "kind," "companionable," and "understanding." The ideal teacher was "fair," "sympathetic," "knew her stuff," and had a sense of humor. The perfect boy, like the perfect girl, was likeable, fun-loving, intelligent, and considerate. The best occupations were those that were "interesting," "satisfying," or "challenging." The worst were the "dull" or "routine" jobs, the ones that required no training or aptitude and had "nothing to offer but money."

Although the prejudiced youngsters repeatedly idealized their parents and often suggested that one's elders knew best, if they could choose one companion with whom they were to be stranded on a desert island, they would never choose a parent but usually one of the gang who could help to ward off danger, or a girl who would "take care of the feeding and home problem." If they had any special problems they thought "the gang" could work them out. In their psychologic tests they unfailingly described all adults in the photographs as punitive or in some way unpleasant. If they saw a picture of a young boy who seemed to be aggressive they would generally spin a story about the punishment that befell him. The passive characters in their tales were invariably attacked because of their weakness.

By contrast, the low prejudiced youngsters often thought they would like to have a parent with them on a desert island; if they had problems they imagined that "talking it over with an older person might help." In their photograph stories the youthful character regularly met challenges, sometimes on his own, sometimes with the help of an older person. More often than not he surmounted his difficulties and was pictured as going on to bigger and better things.

The children were also given a memory test in which a story was read to them describing the behavior of the older pupils toward several newcomers to the school. In the story some of the children were friendly and helpful while others provoked arguments and instigated fighting. The children were then asked to write what they had just heard.

In the versions submitted by the prejudiced youngsters there was marked emphasis upon the fighting incidents: half of them could recall only the unpleasant aspects of the story. Furthermore, they often embroidered their stories so as to develop their goriest aspects, and their final product was a considerable distortion of the original. The youngsters with less prejudice, on the other hand, were far more often able to keep to the original story line and to report both the pleasant and unpleasant incidents more or less as they had heard them.

In another test the children were given a series of photographs of familiar as well as unfamiliar objects and asked to identify each one. The low prejudiced youngsters readily admitted to not knowing or never having seen the strange items. The highly prejudiced youngsters, somehow disturbed by the unknowns and by the necessity for admitting gaps in their knowledge, tried to cover up their ignorance by resorting to wild guesses or giving the unfamiliar object the name of something that "looked a little bit" like it.

In still another and quite independent study, a group of children of approximately equal intelligence were given problem-solving tests. They were shown one possible solution and were then asked to work through several similar problems on their own. The more prejudiced youngsters, with notable frequency, stuck doggedly to the one method that had been demonstrated. As they worked they would display mounting anger and even frenzy over the possibility of failure, but rarely would it occur to them to try a new or different approach. The less prejudiced children, on the other hand, almost immediately set about to find short-cuts, and nothing seemed to please them more than to be able to come up with a variety of solutions that were faster or better than the suggested one.

We have only to dip into the massive evidence available on child development to know that the infant is almost helpless in his violence: that the very young, because of the fright and confusion they are bound to feel over some of life's first experiences, will from time to time react with hostility. It is assumed, however, that as the child grows older some of his earliest fears and confusions will diminish and his behavior will reflect his growing self-confidence. But this can happen only if the child, in addition to *growing*, is also *maturing*.

The evidence would plainly suggest, however, that the prejudiced child is one who is growing in size alone. For underneath his noisy bravado, his excessive bullying or cowing, his intense preoccupation with the gory and the horrible in life, are unmistakable signs of his profound and almost infantile yearning for protection, for comforting walls to shut out his bewilderment, for a refuge to keep him permanently safe from the menacing world.

He is a child who cannot learn the thousand lessons life has to teach him in his growing days, for his mind is so crowded with anxiety that whenever he tries to learn, distrust and unreason hold and torment him. He understands very little about himself and those around him and what little he does understand, as well as the great deal he does not, only intensifies his fright and heightens his misery.

In the young, as in the adult, prejudice is not a simple matter of one person disliking another. It derives from the fact that the child is full of misgivings about himself and therefore full of apprehension about everyone else.

We have looked back upon childhood through the eyes of many now adult, and into childhood through the eyes of many who are there still. We have seen how indelible are those earliest markings; and as we have been able to decipher those that marked the beginnings of fear, we cannot help but become more clearsighted about the beginnings of prejudice as well.

3

The Bitter End: The
Authoritarian Personality

How long a fear can last! And if it has been well buried, how perfectly preserved it appears long after the reasons for it have died!

So many grownups seem to congeal their childhood fears into adult convictions. They translate memories into foregone conclusions repeatedly and the countless things that frightened them in their childhood frighten them still.

The adult who recalls that whenever he had waited for anything as a child, the waiting had ended in punishment or disappointment, now lives in expectation of catastrophe. Waiting for his army assignment, he is certain it will be a wretched one; waiting for his girl, he is sure she will disappoint him. Waiting for a promotion, he is certain it will not come. Waiting for a stranger, he is convinced he will find an enemy.

Because the new experiences in his adult life so often become fused with memories of his first and fearful childhood experiences, these too, seemed preordained to failure. A new job will be linked in his ruminations with the terrifying first day at school; a new girl with the miserably unsuccessful first date; a new home with the unhappy time long ago when his family had to pull up roots and move to a totally strange place.

Because long ago the unknown and unfamiliar had proved consistently terrifying, now all his new adult undertakings frighten much more than they challenge him. For his experience has assured him of nothing but the certainty of misery and failure; and now, whether it is a new feeling or a new face, a new idea or a new place, he is frantic in his efforts to avoid them all.

Since most of the memories of the prejudiced person converge on his unrequited need for protection and belonging, most of his adult thoughts are laced with the desire for safety and security and the determination to exclude others as others had once excluded him. As protection was once his primary object—for all the time he was growing he felt himself to be the helpless victim of the strong and the exploitative—today security remains his chief aim in life and he considers no price too great to pay for it.

But how is he to find this security? How can he be certain that at last he "belongs" unless he can point to many around him who do not? How can he be sure that he is finally on "the inside," unless all around him are those he can quickly identify as "outsiders"?

How is he to identify outsiders? Distinctions must be made: lines must be sharply drawn between those who are like himself and those who are not. Divisions must be defined. If necessary, divisions must be created. And, in any case, divisions must be staunchly maintained. Those who are most like himself are the good, the moral, the diligent. Those who are different are the bad, the immoral, the lazy. Other "clear-cut" distinctions are also necessary: Gentiles must be distinguished from Jews, Protestants from Catholics, white from colored, and yellow from all other colors. White collar workers must be distinguished from laborers, non-union men from union men, workers from bosses. Native born must be distinguished from foreign born; first-generation Americans from fifth-generation Americans—and all Americans from all non-Americans.

The more distinctions one can make, the more exclusions one can urge. The more exclusions one brings about, the more coveted and incidentally the clearer one's own place becomes. For these individuals have no other way of discovering where they *do* belong, except by cataloguing the places where they obviously *do not*. Then they buttress their arguments on the need for exclusions with "evidence," with many alleged "experiences," and with much "personal knowledge." They embroider their documentation with extraneous and irrelevant details, as though by elaborating minutiae they can divert attention from the essence of their distortions.

They use sweeping generalizations and oversimplifications:

"All politicians are corrupt. . . ."

"All business men are out to make a fast buck. . . ."

"All bosses are out to milk the workers. . . .

"All unions are out to break the bosses. . . ."

"All Jews are greedy—the greed is in their bones. . . ."

"All Negroes are untrustworthy—the stealth is in their blood. . . ."

"Alien strains make the foreign born incapable of understanding America the way the purer strains do. . . ."

If they can establish unpleasant traits as ingrained, they can then declare them unalterable; and if they are unalterable, they are also invariable. For even though the prejudiced may occasionally have to admit the possibility of exceptions, these would be the "rarities," and they need be no more interested in them than they are happy about them.

To exclude those who are different from themselves, which is the only road they know to security, they cannot simply criticize some, they must ostracize many. It is understandable, therefore, that they should be eager to see the worst in everyone and be easily persuaded that it is there.

Their search for security, however, must seem as endless as it is hopeless. For they must find it in a world they have convinced themselves is hostile. And they must do this alone, as they have always had to do everything alone, for never in their lives can they remember having had any real help from anyone.

Their greatest handicap by far is that they know so little about security. For they have learned only how elusive and inaccessible it can be. They have seen paradise lost repeatedly, but never have they seen it regained. They cannot begin to imagine, therefore, the countless ways in which security might be achieved, or the numerous places of repose that might be available to them. They could no more identify than they could conceive of the many who would be eager to help them find genuine safety.

It has been observed that endings are often to be seen shaking hands with beginnings, and the scientists maintain that this is what has happened to the individuals we have been describing. Consistently "high" scorers in all their tests, the prejudiced were in every sense the embodiment of the fear and the pessimism that had pervaded their childhood. Because of their constant anxiety, moreover, they perpetually exaggerated the importance of authority. They did not accept only that authority they believed to be justified, they submitted to all authority they believed to be strong. That is why the scientists speak of them as "authoritarian" personalities.

On the other hand, where the beginnings reported were warm and hopeful an authoritarian adult was rarely encountered no matter how grievous his later experiences had been. To be sure, a happy childhood did not always produce a serene adult, but a miserable childhood invariably paved the way for a calamitous adulthood unless somewhere along the way special attention had been given to the understanding, if not to the healing, of earlier wounds.

In view of his own weakness it is understandable that the authoritarian adult should adore power; that while he may be emotional about little else, he might become almost passionate about this. All through the *Studies*, he appeared never really happy unless he was talking of the possibilities of either wielding or submitting to power. For himself, he would declare, he wanted nothing more than to see, and possibly to serve, some "good, strong leaders" (though doubtless he would be happier still if he could find a master so that he might then become a slave.)

Since his concern was primarily with their *strength*, he appeared hardly interested in the *convictions* of the leaders he sought. Where he was going or even why he was going there was of no great moment to him, for his interest was fixed entirely upon who was taking him and who was going along. Since he could not imagine himself possessing authority and not using it against others, he appeared frantic at the thought of power in the hands of those with whom he was not or could not be associated, for he was certain that eventually it would be used against him.

The authoritarian's justification for his love of power was always to be found in his view of life. Prevailing and impending evils were his favorite subjects. He spoke incessantly of violence and disaster, crime and punishment, conflicts between the strong and the weak, the good and the bad. His conversations were dotted with observations concerning the importance of being "realistic," but for him this was simply another way of saying that human nature being what it is, and the world being as it is, what else but chaos can one expect? And what else but massive power could quell such pervasive chaos?

Behind his "realism" there was no hope, only despair; no confidence, only suspicion; not love of mankind, but only acute contempt for it.

The boundaries that separate authoritarian from non-authoritarian personalities are fluid. Encroachments from one side or another are perpetual. There is no such thing, therefore, as the "average authoritarian" any more than there is an "average human being." Nevertheless such personalities have many things in common not only with respect to their past experiences but also in terms of their present behavior.

One of their most insistent needs, for example, is the need to belong. One of their most insistent impulses, therefore, is the impulse to conform. Inevitably, then, they will bear the hallmarks of the society to which they conform and they will have many such marks in common. Authoritarian personalities will resemble one another noticeably in the ways they think and feel and act: to be as much alike as possible is not merely their goal but indeed their only source of security.

In our society, as we remarked earlier, the goals of such individuals receive automatic encouragement. For the premium now is on conformity and the reward for conformity is comfort and belonging. The cost of such comfort, however, is the right to think and to act independently. But to the authoritarian personality this is no cost at all, for his fear of independence greatly exceeds his desire for it, and his need for belonging is more profound than almost any other of his many needs.

It is now generally realized that the impulse to power and the impulse to love are probably the two primary impulses in the lives of all of us. In the tumult of living most of us yield at times to one and at times to the other. Many of us who would regularly choose love find ourselves forced by circumstances to choose power instead; but our choice is usually a deliberate one, and often it is reluctantly pursued.

For the authoritarian personality there are no such problems because there is no such choice. His thoughts are riveted to the need for protection. He neither knows nor has any other goal in life. He is certain that only power can protect him, as only success can buttress him—and his pursuit of both is anything but reluctant.

To gain power and success, however, he must league himself with the people who possess them. Accordingly, he asserts that "those who are down deserve to be down"; "that everyone gets his just deserts"; "that neither the poor nor the weak ought to be coddled." He firmly believes that "financial success is a darn good measure of the man."

Convention is his conscience. He would have little difficulty remaining morally insensible to arson or murder if these were the prevailing customs. Obedience to unjust laws comes as readily as to the just; and even if he could he would probably not bother to distinguish between them.

All the virtues in life are for him reduced to expedience: he looks upon charity as something to be dispensed in Thanksgiving baskets and brotherhood as part of the Sunday Service impinging not at all upon the everyday "practicality" and "toughness" of which he boasts. As one sixteenth-century philosopher has suggested: "He is a Christian because of fear of hell-fire; and if any religion could fright him more he would be of that."

All his earliest miscarriages of love and affection have persuaded him that the exchange of love is at best a wounding mystery. Afraid and uncertain of love, he is also self-conscious about virility. When he speaks of women he speaks of "marriage ties" or obscenity. In his wife he seeks "purity," "sweetness," and housekeeping skills, as though her virtue might cleanse him of his own impurities, real or imagined, and her outer orderliness might somehow diminish the disorder within him. If he speaks of infidelity, he tells of what he has "gotten away with"—not of "unfaithfulness." For tender emotions are alien to him. In fact, the only emotions that are not alien are shame and embarrassment, and these he seems to experience not when he has violated the prevailing mores but only when he has been caught in the violation.

He understands concrete facts and deplores abstract ideas: when he speaks of success it is financial; when he speaks of achievements, they are material. Despite his detachment where people are concerned, he has a marvellous attachment to *things* and the only manifestations of progress he is apt to recognize are the concrete ones. He is excited by new buildings, fine roads, the efficiency of railroads, and the incredible speed of planes, but he is disinterested in the human implications of any of these.

Though he would never admit this and is usually not even aware of it, he longs to break away from all of his present ties but is much too afraid to do so. Therefore he will condemn fiercely the slightest deviation in others. He insists that "to the best of their abilities everyone should live up to the standards that are set for them." He will stoutly maintain that "rebellion is for the young" and that conformity is a sign of maturity.

Like the fearful child who insists upon giving familiar names to unfamiliar objects without regard to their accuracy, he latches on hastily to ready-made opinions because uncertainties make him nervous. He likes things to be "clear-cut," "either black or white." He prefers his ideas in pocket-sized absolutes and even the most perplexing and complicated problems of the day he insists upon describing in just such terms.

Since nothing is more complex than the truth or more intricate than the process by which one must arrive at it, the authoritarian personality is not one to seek it. As a matter of fact, in spite of all his aggressive and self-righteous declarations even he seems to suspect, be it ever so dimly, that his world is structured on falsehoods. He will fight with the last ounce of his strength any move to introduce the truth or any approach to it. For beginning with the way he idealized his parents whom he deeply resents, and ending with the portrait he paints of himself in which he carefully omits all "the bad parts" and lingers lovingly over the good ones, he is the embodiment of deceit. And whereas self-deceit was the beginning, any and all deceits necessary to sustain the initial and central one are eagerly welcomed by him.

Now he flees from ideas as though to be in possession of them might somehow defile him. He truly believes that "too much thinking can cause trouble," that it might even render men impotent, that it usually does make women sexless. He considers that reflection, far from aiding men, is apt to prolong their difficulties. He is violently opposed to "thinking about oneself too much" because, although he does not say and may not even know this, what he fears more than anything else is the discovery and exposure of the misery, loneliness and desolation that are massed inside him.

The dark irony and the deep tragedy of the authoritarian personality have been stated by the Greek philosopher Theophrastus, friend and contemporary of Aristotle: "They are men not easily reformed—because they are so little persuaded of their illness."

There are those who have frankly wondered why, since such authoritarians are the exception and not the rule in our population, so much attention has been focused upon them. Would it not have been more productive, they inquire, to study those who are more representative of most of us—

those who would be neither high nor low on this particular totem pole, but right in the comfortable middle?

Yet, if the authoritarian in our country is so uncommon, how shall we explain the unmistakable echoes he awakens in so many of his countrymen—or the widespread influence this handful of "unrepresentatives" are exerting upon the lives of all the rest of us?

Is it perhaps that there is a core of authoritarianism in all of us, a profound desire to submit to someone, a dark impulse to destroy? In some of us, to be sure, these impulses and desires are better contained than in others, for some of us are more hopeful than others. Where hope is dominant, ancient angers and old pains are not as easily awakened, bitterness and hate are not as quickly unleashed.

The authoritarians we have described may be the exceptional among us. They may be more bitter than most of us. But we must remember that throughout human history it has been from the extremes that leadership has been drawn. It has been the "exceptional" who have saved the world, as it has been the "exceptional"—leading the many "average" —who have time and again plunged it into darkness.

Part Two

The
Devices
of
Fear

———

4

A Place For Some

All of us are plagued by fears; no one is without them. Where we differ from one another is in the extent to which they take possession of us: in the degree of our awareness of them, and in the strange things we do because of them.

Some people, as we have seen, cling frantically to their prejudices to avoid facing their fears. Others try to quiet them with alcohol or to flaunt them in criminal or delinquent exploits. Some even attempt to mask them in a physical ailment. Some succumb to their fears altogether and become mentally ill.

Of all these maladies most of us would consider prejudice, the conversion of fear into hate, as the least calamitous. Yet the American variety of prejudice is far from harmless, and though it may seem more respectable than alcoholism and criminality, it is not really very different from either of these. For all may be flights from one's self and one's fears; and when the journey has ended, the fears will have grown greatly but the fugitive has not grown at all.

Racial and religious prejudice have been known in many different ages and in many different lands; but trained observers of the human scene are increasingly coming to believe that organized persecution at any time or in any place is much more to be explained by the time, the place, and the persecutors than it is by the victims.

In our own time and in our own way of life, for example, prejudice can be socially useful. For each of us is personally governed by two commandments: one is to *"be* good" and the other is to *"make* good." One of course has to do with morality, and the other has to do with one's economic or social position; nevertheless these regularly get in the way of each other. Since in so many aspects of our lives we are matched and rated in comparative terms, often the quickest way up is also the most ruthless one. Generally the best way to achieve recognition for ourselves is to deprecate those around us; and sometimes the only way we can possibly keep ourselves in the clear is to cast shadows on someone else. How much more surefooted we might be in our own struggling ascent if we could hate those we abuse! And if we can prove that the abuse they receive is the abuse they merit —how then can we possibly keep from hating them?

The way many fair-skinned Americans feel about the Negro is a signal illustration of this kind of mental maneuver. For as fear will often breed hate, so does it invite caution as to who and what is to be hated. And whereas all minority groups have traditionally been favored targets, the sociologists tell us that in a country where there are several minority groups, the one most different in appearance from the majority is considered to be the safest target of all. It is also the group, the psychologists tell us, upon whom the majority usually vents its deepest fears.

For many white Americans their deepest fears are those surrounding their determination to be good. Secretly, they would much prefer to express than to repress their primitive impulses: they would rather be lazy than diligent; they might enjoy being dirty once in a while instead of being always fastidiously clean. And certainly there are times when they would prefer to gratify their sex desires instead of controlling them. But they are held tight in the grip of the prevailing Puritan tradition, and early they learned that in our society much more often than not these appetites cannot be satisfied.

They act then as perpetual moderators in the debates between their instincts and their reason. They may succeed in subduing the unacceptable instincts most or even all of the time, but there is always the chance that these might pop up to plague them again and this possibility causes considerable anxiety. The stronger the impulses, moreover, the greater the wish to disown them—and the more difficult it is to do so.

One way to make it *appear* that one is rid of these impulses is to censure them in others—and in fact, in the very act of doing so, one is often helped to curb them in oneself. To call another dirty is to make ourselves—as well as others—conscious of our cleanliness. To call another lazy is to suggest that we are diligent. To denounce another's incontinence renders invisible our own incontinence, real or fantasied.

If those we accuse look as different from us as possible our accusations sound all the more convincing. For if one looks different then is it not to be assumed that he also acts differently? "If *he* possesses such unconscionable traits, then I who am so different from him, most assuredly do *not!*"

Those in search of such a foil would hardly overlook the Negro, for he is eminently qualified on two counts: his difference and his darkness. The Negro is black in a culture that associates blackness with evil and whiteness with purity and goodness. "Dirty black" is so commonly run together that it requires almost a special learning process to separate one word from the other. This is true as well of "light and bright," "pure white," "dark and dreary," and countless other everyday expressions.

Both white and colored youngsters in mixed nursery school classes, it has been noticed, routinely describe colored dolls as "nasty" and "ugly" and white dolls as "pretty" and "nice." At an age when they are ordinarily painstakingly accurate about their colors, the children will call a darker skinned playmate "black," and it is evident from their tone that they are not describing him—they are attacking him.

Because he is dark and he looks, therefore, as though he *might* be evil, many white people project onto the Negro their most troublesome impulses. Like the forbidden instincts of which he reminds them, the Negro then must be "held down" and "kept in his place." The greater the fear of the instincts, the more sternly policed must they be, and the more confining and restricted becomes the "place" designated for the Negro.

When those questioned in the *Studies* thought about the Negro, their thoughts circled incessantly around his moral waywardness. Whether in questionnaire, interview, or psychological tests, Negroes were repeatedly described in terms of their "untamed instincts." They were portrayed as "primitive," as "exceptionally prolific," as "three-quarters animal," as "strange" and "wild." Veterans remembered that Negro soldiers "loved to sleep with white girls the minute they went abroad"; or that "they liked to squander their money on such things as black lace underwear." Negro men, it was frequently asserted, had difficulty "taking their eyes off a good-looking white woman, no matter whom she belonged to."

In a special study of young, white, Anglo-Saxon veterans (to discover whether their war experiences had affected their feelings about minorities) more than half were frankly hostile toward Negroes, and their explanations for this were riveted to the Negroes' alleged immorality. They would take the interviewer the length and breadth of the globe, far beyond their own experience in time or space, to prove how insatiable were the Negroes' physical appetites and how uncontrollable their urges to satisfy them.

Evidence to refute their contentions would be steadfastly rejected. When the interviewer introduced records of outstanding bravery and exceptional fighting on the part of Negroes, these would be dubbed by the prejudiced as "out and out propaganda"; or it was asserted that "the few good fighters" were the exceptions and that there were "damned few at that"; or the Negroes' ability to kill the enemy was seen as consummate proof "of the innate murderer in every last one of them."

Those who were most insistent about imposing restrictions upon the Negro also seemed to be preoccupied with sexual indecencies in others. They were the most eager advocates of stern punishment for all violators of prevailing customs and they urged particularly severe punishment, never treatment, for sex offenders. Generally they agreed with one other statement in the questionnaire, namely: ". . . the sexual orgies of the old Greeks and Romans . . . were nothing compared to some of the goings on in the country today, even in circles where people might least expect to find it."

To be sure, the prejudiced disliked other minorities in addition to Negroes, but more of them were hostile toward Negroes than toward any other group. Some, in fact, concentrated all of their hatred upon them. Moreover, the difference between the prejudice directed at the Negro and that expressed toward other groups was not solely a quantitative difference. For there was a point at which it became qualitative as well and this was the point at which the issue of social equality entered the discussion.

Of 150 middle-class veterans (all previously enlisted men) more than 80 per cent admitted, however reluctantly, that Negroes had their "rights." Close to that number thought that they should have greater educational and employment opportunities and better—though separate—housing. Five out of ten said they would be willing to work next to a Negro on an equal status basis (as compared to nine out of ten who were willing to work with Jews).

When the contemplated equality moved into the more personal areas, however, the statistics all but collapsed. Only one out of ten was willing to live next door to a Negro (although eight out of ten would live next door to a member of a white minority group); and nine out of ten emphatically disapproved of Negroes and whites "mixing together socially."

Those who were opposed to any and all forms of social equality, including integrated housing, appeared to have no difficulty in reconciling their views with their understanding of democracy. "After all," they would declare, "we're not depriving them of anything but the right to mingle with us— and who, after all, wants his sister to marry a Negro? No decent person wants *that* much equality!"

The link between sex fears and hostility toward the Negro came through with shattering intensity in every discussion concerning the status and future of minority groups. For with the white-skinned minorities it was generally conceded, however grudgingly, that eventually they would become an indistinguishable part of the majority. To that end it was suggested that members of these groups ought to shed their "different" customs: that they should learn to dress, to act, and to behave "like everybody else"—the implication being that the sooner this occurred the sooner would their assimilation be achieved.

No such eventuality was remotely considered where the Negro was concerned. In fact, the fear of it provided the ultimate argument in favor of restricting the Negroes' mobility and hence his equality.

In *An American Dilemma,* his comprehensive and penetrating report on the Negro in America, Gunnar Myrdal says of this argument:

In using the danger of intermarriage as a defense for the whole caste system, it is assumed both that Negro men have a strong desire for "intermarriage," and that white women would be open to proposals from Negro men, *if* they are not guarded from even meeting them on an equal plane. The latter assumption, of course, is never openly expressed, but is logically implicit in the popular theory. The conclusion follows that the whole system of segregation and discrimination is justified. Every single measure is defended as necessary to block "social equality" which in its turn is held necessary to prevent "intermarriage."

In his evaluation of this theory Mr. Myrdal states:

The sincerity of the average white person's psychological identification with the "white race" and his aversion to amalgamation
should not be doubted; neither should his attitude that the uphold-
ing of the caste system, implied in the various segregation and
discrimination measures, is necessary to prevent amalgamation. But
the manner in which he constantly interchanges the concepts
"amalgamation" and "intermarriage"—in the meaning of a white
woman's marriage to, or sex relations with, a Negro man—is
bewildering. Amalgamation both in the South and in the North is,
and has always been, mainly a result, not of marriage, but of
illicit sexual relations. And these illicit sex relations have in the
main been confined to white men and colored women. It is further
well known that Negro women who have status and security are less
likely to succumb to sexual advances from white men. Deprivations
inflicted upon Negroes in the South must therefore be a factor tend-
ing to increase amalgamation rather than to reduce it. Together
these facts make the whole anti-amalgamation theory seem incon-
sistent.

Myrdal concludes that "we cannot avoid observing that
*what white people really want is to keep the Negroes in a
lower status,*" and the arguments against social equality are
but rationalizations to achieve this. They may *say*, "no social
equality because this will cause intermarriage." They will
mean, "no intermarriage because this will bring about equality."

Other students of the subject have suggested that since
marriage in our society is a voluntary affair and no one
may be forced to marry another, what the white man really
fears is that white women might *choose* to marry Negroes.
Because they themselves have so consistently pictured the
Negro as highly sexual, some white men cannot quite dispel
the notion that he might therefore be highly desirable.

There is also evidence, drawn from psychological studies, indicating that when he accuses Negroes of wishing to marry or to have sexual relations with white women, a white man may be expressing nothing but his deeply repressed wish to enlarge his own sexual experience. When he calls out so sharply, "*I* am not immoral. *He*, the Negro, is," it is his own guilt he is trying to assuage.

But no matter what the mechanism—whether rationalization or projection—at the heart of it is the conviction that the status of the Negro must not be improved. If the Negro were permitted to leave his "place," the prejudiced white man could no longer be certain of his own position; for he finds his place only by keeping others in theirs, and he proves himself only by declaring his superiority over them. Should these others become free they might also become equal, and then the prejudiced could be certain of nothing at all—unless it were utter bewilderment and chaos.

Projection, displacement, rationalization—these may have been named by our contemporary scientists but they were not discovered by them. It was a long time ago that Aesop set down his "sour grapes" fable; and it is stated in the Bible that "wherein thou judgest another, thou condemnest thyself." These mental maneuverings have been responsible for some of the crueler inhumanities men have practiced upon each other throughout all of history. And today they continue to be responsible for many of the inhumanities Americans practice upon one another.

Essentially projection is a kind of frame-up, and the only way it differs from the underworld frame-up is that the one doing the framing is not aware of what he is doing. In purpose and effect, however, they are identical: both are devices for saving oneself and both victimize others without regard to their guilt or innocence.

In some ways projection also resembles the ancient pagan ritual of scapegoating. Then, it will be remembered, the people unburdened their sins onto a goat and dispatched animal and load into the wilderness to perish. But there the unburdening process was deliberate; and the victim was a goat and not another human.

It was the unconscious character of projection, we will recall, that made the photograph tests employed in the *Studies* so useful. For in every instance the stories that were attributed to the pictures were utterly and innocently self-centered. So clearly did they reveal the private woes and worries of the narrator that they assumed the character of uncensored, though disguised, confessions. Since none of the participants knew what he was revealing, these projective tests regularly provided investigators with important leads into regions of the mind that might otherwise have remained uncharted.

Another of the studies based upon case histories of patients undergoing psychotherapy provided further evidence of the extraordinary faithfulness of projection. For the patients invariably tagged others with the traits and conflicts that were most disturbing to themselves. The link between their private despair and the anger they directed toward others was never evident to them.

One patient, for example, suffered deep anxieties over his failure to hold a job and to provide adequately for his family. He was particularly angered by Jews because "it was uncanny the way they managed to take care of themselves"; because they were "materialistic" and "overambitious"; "because they always look after their own." Another patient anguished by his sexual impotence appeared profoundly un-nerved by people whom he imagined to be "constantly over-indulging themselves." He disliked Jews "because of the intensity of their emotions" and their "sensualness." He detested Negroes because "all they ever think about is sex."

The image these people held of all whom they hated was consistently refracted through their own fears. Once they were made aware of those fears, their views of others were altered accordingly.

But in an underworld frame-up the real culprit usually considers it sufficient merely to "pin the goods" on his dupe and then skip town, or simply wait it out. In our psycho-logical frame-ups we not only arrange for our victim's con-viction, *we insist upon it and even carry it out.*

Considering the nature of the frame-up so frequently per-petrated upon the Negro, this consequence is not at all sur-prising. For the prejudiced project on to him all their own most alarming impulses—certainly those around which the taboos are heaviest. Small wonder then that they should be unable to look at the Negro without a feeling of alarm and that, in their disturbance, they should often be joined by the most respected individuals and institutions in society. For no responsible educator, no worthy churchman, no decent com-munity or self-respecting member of the community can afford to remain impassive in the face of moral laxity.

Thus the prejudiced can feel guiltless and even virtuous about their maltreatment of the Negro. Condemning the Negro, moreover, is not only cleansing, it is elevating, for to proclaim another's inferiority makes one's own superiority all the more apparent.

The prejudiced may not be aware of the reasons that impel him to put the Negro in his place, but his efforts to keep him there are quite deliberate. For these have more to do with economic and political needs than with psychological ones, and with social as well as individual pressures.

There is much to be gained from the continued submergence of a whole group of people. To benefit from prejudice, moreover, one need not even share it: in fact those who have used it most effectively, economically or politically in our own and in other countries, have been those who recognized its existence in others and used it as they would any other weapon to achieve their objectives.

It is now generally recognized, for example, that the reason the Negro was more methodically submerged in the South than in the North after his "emancipation" was not because he was more hated there but because he was more needed there. It was essential to the success of the plantation system that a great reservoir of cheap labor be available and the suppression of the Negro swiftly accomplished this. In the South today industry continues to benefit from its lower wage rates traceable in large measure to the submerged state of the Negro.

In the North, in states where legislation does not prohibit it, there are still some firms and business institutions that boast a "restricted" personnel policy and these are often also the places that offer lower wages. The more restricted the hiring policy, the more "elite," presumably, are the ones who work there. Those whose need for prestige is great enough—and who have no other way of acquiring it—are often glad to accept less money for the privilege of such an association.

Then, of course, there are those who in order to make their own lives bearable need to have and to hold their prejudices. For no matter how much the idea may dismay us, when we are miserable—unless we are saints—most of us find an odd comfort in the knowledge that there are others whose misery surpasses our own. In the South, for example, for long years after the Civil War the poor whites would have had nothing had they not had the poorer Negroes. Today, in both North and South, there are those who find it comforting and even necessary to know that there are some whom they can declare to be their inferiors.

There are then many psychological and economic reasons for the suppression of the Negro but these are neither audible nor visible in the explanations given by the prejudiced. The reasons reside in the white men and in American society itself; but the explanations are uniformly affixed to the Negro.

It was said by the prejudiced in all the *Studies* that the Negroes were "child-like"; that as they shared none of the restraints of decent people neither did they share their social or economic ambitions. Negroes, it was claimed, are happy the way they are.

It was said that the Negroes are dirty and take no pride in their appearance; that they are innately stupid—fit for nothing but the most menial tasks. It was maintained that Negroes have "no sense of values," that they "lack self-respect," that they are hapless and planless. Even such virtues as the Negro was alleged to possess—his love of children, his enjoyment of the "simple pleasures," the "animal-like" devotion of which he was presumed to be capable—

these were used to support, never to challenge, what was implicit in all such arguments, namely, that for the Negro, slavery is a perfect vocation.

In the more extensive interviews, and in response to deliberate prodding by the interviewers, the arguments often shifted. Where before the Negro was contemptible because of his weakness, now he was insufferable because of his arrogance. Where before he was hopelessly stupid, now he was dangerous when he is educated for then "nothing is good enough for him." Where before the Negro was without ambition and eminently content with his lot, now it was argued that "he wants nothing more than to be where the whites are." "Give him a finger and he'll take a hand." "Give him a job with whites and the first thing you know the colored are taking over and the whites are out on the street."

It mattered little what exactly was said as long as somehow the notion was kept alive that the Negro *deserves* his confinement. It is as though having determined to treat him as a subordinate the prejudiced would now authorize this treatment by proving that he *is* one. "Haughty nation," George Bernard Shaw said of America not so long ago, "they make the Negro clean their boots and then prove his inferiority by the fact that he is a boot-polisher."

Only the intensity with which the prejudiced defends his arguments suggests how vital they are to him. It is as though by some dim premonition he had begun to suspect that what he is really defending is himself; for only as long as he can keep the Negro in his place can the preeminence of his own place go unchallenged. Only as long as the Negro is nobody can he, the prejudiced, be somebody.

Actually, when the highly prejudiced and those low in prejudice talked about the Negro, they did not differ greatly in their description of his present condition. They moved apart sharply, however, in their explanations for it.

When those low in prejudice looked at the Negro they perceived instantly the deviltry of discrimination. When the prejudiced observed him, they saw only conclusive proof of his inferiority. "People get what they deserve," we will remember, is the philosophy to which the prejudiced person is especially devoted—and he applies it relentlessly to everyone but himself.

"Highs" and "lows" also differed in their prophecies with respect to the Negro's future in American life. Those relatively unprejudiced were often surprisingly gloomy when they thought about the matter. Although they generally urged immediate measures to equalize education and employment opportunities, suggesting that once this were to happen "the other things would take care of themselves," they rarely failed to mention the serious difficulties in the way of any really satisfactory solution.

The highly prejudiced on the other hand were often blandly optimistic. They regularly predicted that "everything would work out some day," thus simultaneously shedding their guilt and their responsibility. For the "day" was invariably not in our lifetime nor even in the foreseeable future, and what the prejudiced person was saying in effect was that he for one did not intend to do anything about the matter in *his* lifetime. Sometimes gravely, sometimes impatiently, he would suggest that "these things need plenty of time." Always he would advise "caution," "patience"—and above all "realism."

"Realism," to be sure, means different things to different people, but we must remember that to the prejudiced "reality" bespeaks not hope but despair, not faith in humankind but only contempt for it. When he pleads for time, therefore, it is not because he either hopes or believes that time will prove him wrong, but because he hopes and believes that in time he will be proven an oracle, and his prejudices will be recalled as the inspired prophecies of a sage.

It is likely that what the prejudiced considers to be his normal vision would be regarded as partial vision by anyone else. Yet his impairment is purposively acquired. He misses a great deal that way to be sure, but that is precisely why he enjoys it. For no matter what he is observing he does not have to see everything that is there *but only what he is looking for*.

When the prejudiced person observes the Negro, the evidence he is looking for all but leaps at him. He can assert with calm, as he can document with confidence, the fact that Negroes "are forever getting into trouble." Now he can hide his hatred behind solemn sociological discourses on the extent of the Negro's misbehavior. He can produce irrefutable evidence that a disproportionate number of them figure in nation-wide statistics of crime, delinquency, and broken homes. Among Negro children he can easily find alarming evidence of waywardness and mental retardation. Among Negro adults he can demonstrate repeated failures at jobs that were "over their heads."

There is an appalling truth in everything he says. But the truth that transcends all the others is that Negroes do not start out that way. Where it exists their inferiority is acquired, not inherited. It reflects imperfect education, not impaired intelligence; it reflects limited opportunities and aborted hopes, not inborn incompetence. Above all it reflects the stinging experience of having been born a member of a dispossessed group.

Hearing so much about the American dream but so rarely sharing in it, the Negro knows only the creed his experience has taught him: "With liberty and justice for all—except me." The creed he has learned might easily breed in him arrogance, bitterness, laziness, and shiftlessness—and even a burning desire to earn a "fast buck" to make up for the opportunities he lacks to earn an honest one.

If the Negro often seems to be molded in the image his enemies have of him, it is not because that image is either preordained or immutable. It is because when those who hold the image are both numerous enough and powerful enough, they are actually able to breathe life into it.

It is said that men begin to resemble that which they live with most intimately. The American Negro lives in painful intimacy with the notion of his inferiority. It is in his history and in his present being. It is on the lips of those who raise him and in the faces of those who deal with him, in the epithets that are hurled at him, and the numberless places that refuse him entry. It is in the roles in which he is cast in films, plays, and novels. It is sealed in the unmistakable reality of his inferior job and his inferior home.

But it is not inborn in him. Countless studies of pre-school youngsters both colored and white have revealed that—given comparable health and environmental situations—the children prove equal in intelligence. Moreover at pre-school age Negro youngsters regularly reveal character traits vastly different from the stereotype of Negro adults: they are sensitive, quick, ambitious, and energetic.

But as early as three, many are deeply disturbed by their color. They describe themselves as "not dark but light" and they beg their parents to "wash their skins clean." Fiercely they reject the colored dolls, and when the choice is theirs to make they regularly choose white youngsters for their playmates. Whether he is three or four or only two when he makes his discovery, by the time the Negro child discovers his color he has also discovered the stigma attached to it.

By seven or eight, Negro children no longer innocently deny their pigmentation and frequently they appear to have made a truce with it. How uneasy is that truce is evident by the way they go about choosing their friends from among those whose skins match their own. Only the intensity of the quarrels that break out amongst them suggests their deep-lying despair and unhappiness. It is almost as though, even at this age, their gnawing self-contempt is being subtly translated into contempt for one another.

By that time too, their intellectual performance often fails to live up to the promise of the intelligence they earlier revealed. Progressively then, year after year, the gap between achievement and ability may be seen to widen until it becomes so great that children and teachers alike, anxious to dodge the painful implication, prefer to believe there is no gap at all and that the performance is inferior because the Negro child is inferior.

Unlike the deprivation of those who most hate him, the Negro's deprivation is not imaginary. He does not *suppose* that the world in which he lives is a cold and hostile place, he *knows* it. For almost the first thing the Negro child learns is the importance of controlling his anger—of concealing everything and revealing nothing of the way he truly feels. Negro parents regularly assert that early in their children's lives they try to teach them how to "behave themselves" in order "to keep out of trouble": to sacrifice truth, if necessary, for social harmony.

Unlike his persecutors, however, the Negro does not find it easy to deceive himself. In fact he detests it; and he detests even more the necessity for practicing deceit on others in order that he may survive.

The Negro's condition is changing, of course, and so will the Negro as he comes to trust the permanence of that change. But until now he has been aware that much of his advancement was mothered by necessity—not his, but the white man's. He remembers that only when the need for combat reinforcements was desperately urgent was he permitted to fight alongside of white soldiers. He knows that, in skilled and professional jobs, more often than not he is the last to be hired, and he cannot help believing that he will also be the first to be fired. Inside him always is the grinding fear that the same opportunism that was responsible for his gains may one day be responsible for his losses.

Decisions of the highest court and increasing legal guarantees implicit in burgeoning legislation are beginning to dissolve his fears. But for a long while it is to be expected that the Negro will waver uncertainly between equality and inferiority, feeling barely qualified for either. He will have only to look back to know how far he has come; but he will have only to look forward to know how far he must travel in his fight against the remaining inequalities. In the trek he has yet to make his memories warn him that at best he will find tolerance, at worst outright rejection; and more likely he will find merely sufferance. Acceptance is something he hardly dares to hope for.

But acceptance is what the Negro needs most of all. For if others continue to think of him as unacceptable, then he must continue to think of himself in the same way. If he cannot accept himself neither can he respect himself. Lacking self-respect and personal dignity he will be unable to use wisely or well the long-awaited opportunities he so greatly deserves, and that now at last are beginning to be available to him.

In the early days of our country when European critics were carping over our failure to achieve distinction, Jefferson's reply to them was simple: "Let us come into existence," he said, "before being asked to justify our existence."

The selective vision of the highly prejudiced serves him well. He sees only sinners and savages, and one is *expected* to bar them from the company of the civilized and the virtuous. If one sees victims and suffering, one is expected to help. But the prejudiced cannot really help anyone until he begins to help himself. For if he had been able to reduce his own torment in the first place he would not now be finding it necessary to torment others.

But even though out of his own need the prejudiced may be impelled to defy the American creed and all of its teachings, he does not ever totally reject them. His country's heritage and tradition of "liberty and justice for all," including Negroes, exercises an authority over him as it does over any other American. And what makes any one of us writhe inwardly is not the knowledge that we have hurt another but that we were wrong to do so. In the presence of injustice, therefore, fear is always particularly wakeful. "If the white man fears the Negro," said Booker T. Washington, "it must be because he does not intend to deal with him justly."

The fear that induced the white man's prejudice has grown because of it. The added fear strengthens the prejudice; the prejudice reinforces the restrictions; the restrictions increase the resentment of the Negro and multiply the guilt of the white man. The chain is now complete. Its ends are looped; and it shackles equally all who helped to forge it.

5

A Wall Against Others

> There are two ways of looking at the wall
> between Jews and Gentiles; from the inside
> and from the outside. On the one hand it can
> be said that the actual masonry is done by
> the Jews: the Jews mix the mortar and lay the
> bricks and complain about the wall but are
> sometimes glad to have it. On the other hand
> it is the Gentiles who oblige the Jews to build
> the wall and who supply most of the materials
> for it, and they are very smug about its
> existence; without ever going inside it they
> assume it is better to be outside and to keep
> the Jews inside.
>
> —from *The Wall*, by JOHN HERSEY

Those whose fears impel them to hate are rarely satisfied with
one hate and generally have no difficulty sustaining quite a
few simultaneously. Such people, however, often have a "pet
hate" and this, as we might now suspect, is almost always
associated with their "pet fear." Some, for example, are
much more anxious about *making* good than about *being*
good: economic insecurity troubles them far more than the

restlessness of their instincts. Apparently such people find the Jew an especially inviting quarry.

The stereotypes that prevail with respect to the Jews are so numerous and resilient that anyone thrashing around for reasons to justify his ill feeling would have no trouble finding among them something that especially appealed to him. Jews are disliked because they are bankers or because they are beggars; because they are revolutionaries or all-powerful industrialists; because they are "too clannish" or because they are "forever trying to get in where they don't belong"; because they are too intellectual or too business minded; too material or too spiritual; too weak or too strong. But although the charges hurled at them are shot through with contradictions, there are some that seem to recur with particular fervor and frequency.

Whereas the Negro was most often attacked in the *Studies* for such unenviable qualities as his physical violence or moral abandon, the Jew was most often censured for his economic power or his excessive intellectuality. Whereas the Negro was upbraided for lacking such solid American virtues as thrift, ambition, and shrewdness, the Jew was condemned for possessing these virtues to an excessive degree. In short, where hostility against the Negro was routinely rationalized so as to justify *holding him down,* attacks against the Jew seemed more often calculated to *pull him down* from an exalted economic or intellectual position.

But the "uncanny superiority" of the Jew—like the "innate inferiority" of the Negro—regularly turned out to be an image perceived through the lens of fear. In fact the American variety of anti-Semitism seems to have much more in common with other forms of American prejudice than it does with anti-Semitism in other ages and in other lands.

It is true that Jews have been persecuted in slave and feudal societies, in capitalist countries and in Communist lands. The reasons for their persecution, however, differed in each instance; for they were both time-conditioned and place-conditioned.

In the pre-Christian era the Jews were caught up in the conflicts of the ancient nations because they lived along the major trade routes and in the vitally strategic areas of the Old World. In the Christian era they were a conspicuous non-Christian minority at a time when the Church was a dominant force throughout Europe. Also, the conflict between Judaism and Christianity was acutely sharpened by the paradox of the Christians' worship of Christ and the Jews' denial of Him although He had been a Jew.

In the fifth century and for some thirteen centuries thereafter Jews were deprived of their citizenship. Although this was initially an act of religious intolerance, it had far-reaching political and social consequences, for they could no longer be a part of the body politic wherever they resided. In medieval times, having no legal rights, they lived in cities only at the pleasure of the princes. They were barred from owning property, excluded from most occupations and from artisan guilds. The ruling potentates employed them as tax collectors and in that capacity they were required to force payments out of reluctant citizens.

By the tenth century the development of commerce and the growth of cities brought more and more Christians into occupations and trades in direct competition with Jews. As citizens and members of the dominant religious group Christians could and often did order the expulsion of Jews in great numbers from the cities of western Europe. In eastern Europe, where many sought refuge, their fate was much the same. They continued to be barred from citizenship, blocked from most occupations, and subjected to periodic attacks of personal violence.

All of these events, as Professors Simpson and Yinger of Oberlin College point out in their recent and comprehensive analysis of *Racial and Cultural Minorities,* served to throw the Jews back upon themselves, to perpetuate them as a cohesive religious-cultural group and to enhance their differences from the rest of the people in those lands where they resided without being accepted. They also point out that once a group has been set apart as a target for hostility it is chosen more readily for that purpose the next time "because tradition suggests it, guilt feelings demand it, and perhaps, the responses of the minority group . . . encourages it."

In recent years historians, theologians, social and political scientists have all called attention to the extraordinary usefulness of anti-Semitism for the totalitarian-minded. In totalitarian countries where people are surfeited with fear and anxiety, ways must be found to divert their attention from their own giant-sized and often insoluble problems. Since these people cannot attack with impunity the real cause of their difficulties—usually the man or the party in power—and since their leaders wish at all costs to avoid uprisings, leaders and followers alike will gladly join forces for a diversionary attack.

In those countries Jews have frequently been the target for such attacks because they were continuously available.

Moreover, they possess several obvious qualifications for the role of scapegoat: they are numerically fewer than the majority and therefore not likely to attempt retaliation; they are distinguishable from the majority because of their different customs and places of worship; and finally, it can always be stated that others have also victimized them. For the persecutory-minded there can be no more convincing arguments than these. They provide him with all the evidence he needs to agree that their further persecution is now in order.

But do such explanations apply as well to America and Americans? For in our country hostility to Jews must exist in defiance, not in support, of officially pronounced doctrines. Ironically, this very fact provides the American anti-Semite with one of his favorite arguments. "If even in *this* country Jews feel the barbs of prejudice," they contend, "it must be because they invite it." "If there is anti-Semitism even in America," the prejudiced often maintain, "then the Jews can only blame themselves."

As the scientists explored the depth and breadth of the anti-Jewish prejudice extant in our country their findings revealed a noticeable tie-up between economic anxiety and anger toward Jews. But it was also noticeable that such anxiety was traceable not to facts but to feelings. Some of those who were most unhappy and most anxious about the future were holding more lucrative positions than they had ever held and confessed to being better situated financially than they had ever been. Yet for one reason or another they persisted in their lamentations.

Among one group of veterans in similar occupations, some

were consistently optimistic and others were just as consistently dour and fretful. The unhappy ones, moreover, were unhappy not only about their future but about their recent army experiences, the inadequacy of their present pensions, the government's failure to "do right" by the vets who had "sacrificed so much." And prominent in their list of complaints there were always some concerning Jews, Negroes, and any other minority that popped into mind.

On the other hand, there were many who had seen active fighting and even some who had sustained serious injuries, but who nonetheless had fewer complaints about the army or the government. Far from worrying about the future they were confident that they would always be able "to get along somehow." In short they were philosophic about the future as they were about the present and the past—and this general amiability reflected itself as well in their feelings about people, including, specifically, people who were members of minority groups.

There seemed little doubt but that the economic insecurity so characteristic of the highly prejudiced was related not to present circumstances but to remembered ones; and further study usually revealed that the memories that provoked their anxiety were not of economic deprivation but of emotional impoverishment. Some of the most insecure adults appeared to have grown up in homes where there had been ample money but a great deal of worry surrounding it. On the other hand many of those who were now quite serene remembered chronic shortages of funds in their childhood but no serious family disturbances because of that fact. Usually they would recall numerous other satisfactions that "money couldn't have bought."

In the childhood of all the prejudiced and economically insecure there were some commodities that had been far scarcer than money, namely, warmth and affection, tenderness and understanding; and it was startling to see how persuasive those earliest memories could be. For the adults who recalled mainly desolation and deprivation in their youth seemed to find it exceedingly difficult to feel anything but deprived and desolate many years later, no matter how much improved were their circumstances.

The evidence is insistent. Economic insecurity often goes hand in hand with unhappiness about Jews—but when it does, the insecurity is as little caused by economics as the unhappiness is caused by Jews.

The prejudiced, of course, believed otherwise. In their minds there was little doubt but that many of the ills that befell them and their country were in large measure traceable to Jews or to the influence of Jews.

They upbraided the Jews for their "craftiness," for their "shrewdness," for the way they "stuck together," accumulating money and power "all for their own." They decried their "pushiness," their ambition, their drive, their inclination to seek out "intellectual" instead of "physical" occupations: "When it comes to doing an honest day's work with their hands instead of their heads, the Jews are never anywhere to be seen. . . ."

Once they fastened on to one disagreeable trait, moreover, they found no difficulty in extending their list indefinitely. If the Jews were alleged to be powerful it was obvious that they must have achieved this power by dishonest means. If they were dishonest economically, they soon became dishonest politically, hence they "controlled" important areas of national government policy, and shortly it was clear that they were "international plotters." If Jewish soldiers fought in the front lines they were "killers." If they did not they were "connivers" who managed to get themselves "the cushy jobs because they were all cowards anyway." If the Jews were emotional in their relations with one another, they then were also "overly-sensual"—and they liked nothing more than "to take advantage of Gentile girls."

As the alcoholic finds his second drink easier to excuse than the first—and all drinks thereafter easier still—so the prejudiced person seemed to have no trouble embellishing his case against the Jews, once he had decided to construct one. As it turned out, however, his case revealed much more about himself than it did about his declared enemies.

For the very persons who were most scathing about the "money-mindedness," the "grasping" and "acquisitive" nature of the Jews, had agreed emphatically with the questionnaire statement that "financial success is an important measure of the man," that "every child should learn the value of money early," and that "the business man is more important to society than the artist." High on the list of men they most admired were business men and industrialists: ". . . men like Ford and Morgan . . . because they kept their noses to the grindstone" and they "knew the value of the dollar."

Both the highly prejudiced and those low in prejudice often included Abraham Lincoln among their heroes, the "lows" explaining their choice in terms of his "humanitarianism," his understanding of and sympathy for the people; while the prejudiced applauded his "ceaseless ambition," his "phenomenal struggle from penniless beginnings to the most powerful position in this country," his "prudence," and his "thrift"—because these were the qualities that had helped him "to succeed against great odds."

In the study drawn from case histories of individuals undergoing psychotherapy, the patient's anti-Jewish feelings frequently provided important clues to his own conflicts and difficulties. Such patients often complained of "aimlessness," of not knowing where they "belonged"; they suffered from a sharp sense of failure and appeared generally overwhelmed by their own inadequacies. When these people attacked Jews for their "strong family ties," their "confounded loyalty to each other," or their "uncanny ability to succeed," it was not so much because they objected to these traits in Jews, as because they missed them so profoundly in themselves. In a desperate attempt to bolster themselves they would try to make these attributes appear grotesque; or they would attribute the Jews' success to dishonesty, or to "craftiness," hoping that then their own failure to make good might seem less disgraceful.

But whatever the mental device and whatever the reasons for it, it was apparent from his own testimony that there were no qualities the prejudiced admired more than "burning ambition," "smartness," "push," and "know-how." For all who possessed them he was filled with envy and veneration—unless the possessors happened to be Jews, and then he was filled only with anger.

The prejudiced also talked a good deal about the Jews' "difference"—the "strangeness" that shrouded all of them and made it impossible "to ever *really* get close to any one of them." Some alleged that they could always identify a Jew because there was an "unmistakable something about all of them. . . ."

But the very ones who said this were most indignant during their interviews about the Jews who were "forever changing their names," or having "plastic surgery performed on their noses," for "it was getting so that you never knew anymore when one was sitting right next to you." Often these were the same people who objected to the "light Negroes," because they were "always passing themselves off as whites."

The adults who were most critical of Jews for not behaving like everybody else were also the ones who insisted in their questionnaire that "no matter how Americanized a Jew might seem to be, there is always something different and strange, something basically Jewish underneath. . . ." Their proposals to solve "the Jewish problem" were embroidered around the necessity for Jews to make themselves less obtrusive—to avoid "going where they're not wanted" and to "stop trying to imitate Gentiles."

They would require, in short, that the Jews cease trying to be different but also stop trying to act like Gentiles; that they learn to behave like everybody else—but that one must realize that they cannot, really, because "a Jew never loses his Jewishness"; that they become thoroughly Americanized, but that one must be careful about allowing them in everywhere for too many Jews in a neighborhood, in a school, in a business, and even in the country, might have "dire consequences" for all concerned.

It was patently clear, in other words, that those most insistent that the Jews liquidate their Jewishness, would be the very ones who would instantly make it impossible for them to do so.

Precisely because it is so immersed in irrationality, American anti-Semitism has sometimes been described as a festering social disease. Some have gone so far as to suggest that those who succumb to it are themselves emotionally ill. The evidence yielded from the *Studies*, however, does not entirely support such a thesis.

It is true that the extremely hostile individual appeared to be bursting with anxieties he could neither admit nor identify, frightened by weakness he constantly disclaimed, haunted by loneliness that sent him perpetually in search of a crowd. His mind seemed to be heavily stocked with those things he needed to sustain the image of his superiority. Of his hatreds and all the reasons he gave for them, fear was unmistakably the inventor.

Such a person is obviously deeply disturbed—but he is not necessarily "ill." Without his prejudices it is possible that he might become so; for once he can no longer pay absorbed attention to the faults of everyone else he might find time to take a look at himself, and the sight might well plunge him into abysmal despair. His prejudices are often the most important armor he has against himself and the world. It is not surprising, therefore, that he cares for them so deeply. Without them he would be almost entirely defenseless.

The inner disturbance of the highly prejudiced is not necessarily visible to the naked eye. For his nervous need for reassurance impels him to frantic efforts to behave like everyone else. He often takes particular pains with his dress, for example, for he is extremely sensitive to appearances. He cultivates manners rather than kindness. He is guided by example rather than by reason. His actions are rarely the product of understanding or conviction, they are simply an imitation of what "most people" do. In fact the prejudiced is frequently to be found wedged in among "the best people" —but only he knows that truly he is not a part of them. Only he knows how faltering is his confidence in himself and everyone around him and only he is aware of the vexation he feels because of this.

To those who see him merely in passing, however, he often appears precisely the way he wishes to appear, namely, very much like anyone else; and far from seeming disturbed, therefore, he often seems well adjusted indeed to his surroundings!

Then too, just as all disturbed people are not necessarily prejudiced people, neither are all the prejudiced necessarily disturbed. There are some whose animus is more to be explained by inertia than by insecurity. It is the result of an indiscriminate "soaking up" of prevailing stereotypes and existing biases. These are individuals who are either too lazy, too indifferent, or too timid to separate fact from fiction, and who therefore prefer the ready-made slogans of others to the painful effort of reasoned and independent thinking.

As with the Negro, our atmosphere is heavy with unsavory stereotypes and traditions concerning Jews. In everyday language the word "Jew" is still used by some as a synonym for "usurer" or as a colloquialism for ruthless bargaining. In literature, in art and in the theater the Jews have been portrayed repeatedly as evil and uncouth, sharp-featured penny-pinchers. In history and legend they have been depicted as wandering from country to country, unwanted wherever they went, aliens wherever they settled. The artistic vilification of them begun in medieval frescoes and portals, in hymnals and prayer books, in passion plays and miracle plays, has been serenely perpetuated by contemporary religious artists and producers (some of whom are themselves Jews), and by cartoonists and lampooners as well. Millions in our country who have never seen a Jew "know" from a stream of stories, jokes, and old wives' tales what they can expect should they some day chance to meet one.

But none of these things actually *cause* prejudice unless the inclination is there to begin with. If the predilection to hate is there, then tradition will certainly seem to sanction it, and everywhere one turns the environment will be found to encourage it. But if neither the will nor the wish to hate exist, then the same tradition might provoke anger or shame, if it provoked anything. The hostile environment might go unnoticed, but should it be noticed, it would not go unchallenged.

Since in America no one is required to hate Jews and officially no one is expected to, "to be or not to be" an anti-Semite is a personal decision. Some having strong feelings about the matter will follow their own inclinations regardless of the views of those around them. For many Americans, however, the decision to attack or to defend Jews, to avoid them or to befriend them, is likely to have more to do with prevailing custom and fashion than with any deep-lying convictions.

This is also true to some extent where Negroes are concerned. But there, we will remember, it is much more often assumed that no one would be censured for admitting one's dislike or even for proposing that "reasonable" restrictions be enforced. In some places, in fact, this is the expected and approved view, and any apparent disharmony between such views and democratic principles is easily rationalized in terms of the danger of intermarriage that is regularly seen to attend the dropping of the color line.

But when it comes to open expressions of anti-Semitism our country's boiling point is somewhat lower. For there are not the obvious and ready-made justifications for hostility that exist with respect to the Negro. The Jews are not black, and often they are not different from everyone else. Their most "galling" characteristics are not always considered objectionable in American life—and all but the extremely prejudiced are to some extent aware of these facts.

Anti-Semitism therefore must be much more subtly expressed if it is not to tangle with the sensibilities of the many who will not countenance it. Thus it is more often than not masked in good manners, and sometimes it is even more painstakingly disguised. Often an attack upon Jews is neatly concealed in what professes to be a defense of them. What has happened to Jews, it will be declared, is surely deplorable, no matter how justified. And forthwith all further remarks are devoted to justifying and none at all to deploring.

Their long history of persecution, for example, was often cited as "regrettable"—but also as something to excuse its continued existence: "anything that's gone on *that* long is not going to get fixed overnight. . . ." ". . . after all, we cannot expect suddenly to reverse the tide of history."

The "some of my best friends" argument is useful because it implies so clearly that a few exceptions can hardly be expected to alter the rule.

Discussion of the Jew's "somehow different" and therefore "prejudice-forming" behavior quietly ignores the fact that where this behavior does exist, it is more a result than a cause of prejudice. Even if it were not, nothing could be more alien to the concept of American democracy than the notion that difference *per se* is a proper ground for prejudice.

In circles where it is adjudged a mark of urbanity to exclude Jews it is considered a mark of even greater urbanity to say nothing about it—in the same sense that a "gentlemen's agreement" among realtors implies not only an agreement to refrain from selling property to Jews but the "gentlemanliness" of it as well.

Anti-Semitism of this polite variety—and this was by far the most common of all forms uncovered in the *Studies*—is often reasoned, frequently garbed in intellectuality, and generally offered in the reflective tones of justice. Violence is always eschewed: "Hitler's methods were unthinkable—no matter what provocation the Jews may have given. . . ." Though "a different breed, Jews after all, are human"; though "they may invite the trouble they get there are civilized ways of dealing with them."

Some suggested that Jewish leaders should be given the responsibility for "making their people less offensive." If Jews cannot or will not police "their own" then Gentiles may have to; that would be regrettable, of course, but the Jews would have "only themselves to blame" for such an eventuality. Self-imposed social restrictions were suggested, also, presumably, in the Jews' own best interests since "most of them prefer to be among themselves anyway. . . ."

Those who spoke in this vein would have been profoundly shocked had they learned how "high" were their scores on the Anti-Semitism Scale. For they were never arrogant and they were always careful to qualify anything they did say about Jews:

"I feel very different about them than I do about Negroes; . . . after all they're white and much more human. . . ."

"I don't consider myself prejudiced and actually I feel very strongly that Jews have their rights, but at the same time . . ."

"I really have nothing against them . . . in fact I know quite a few Jews who would agree with me. . . ."

These were all people who were keenly aware of the import of individual rights and often it was upon this principle that their appeal ultimately came to rest: *their* "right to choose" those with whom they would work, live, and play.

Given bland skies and an encouraging breeze, however, we should not be at all surprised to find the polite anti-Semite sailing serenely, and not at all unwillingly, into a harbor of hate.

To be sure, not all the hostile were so guarded in their sentiments. Some would begin by proclaiming that they had nothing against Judaism: it was only Jews they disliked. They would then proceed to list the reasons why they, personally, didn't care much for Jews, and in no time at all they were busy proving why Jews should not be liked by anyone. Supporting evidence—no matter how tattered or contradictory—was tossed about airily; stereotypes were grist to the mill. Evidence refuting their arguments was ignored or denied. The more violent their hostility, the more dangerous would they make the Jew appear; for only a coward takes on a weak adversary. The more persecutory, the more reasons one must find for the persecution.

The discourse of the outspoken anti-Semite was laced through with the necessity for self-protection. He appeared perpetually poised to defend himself and the Gentile world from being overrun and overwhelmed by Jews. None dare rest, he would insist, because of the power concentrated in the hands of Jews. Certainly *he* would not rest until this menacing power was placed where it properly belonged—in the hands of the Gentiles.

When he had worked his way through all the stereotypes he could think of, he was likely to summarize his position with something resembling the observation that "no matter how you cut it or what you say, there's something about Jews [or Judaism] that gives me the creeps."

A surprising number of these plainspoken Jew-haters, however, were equally blunt about their aversion toward their own religion. Many asserted proudly that they had not been inside a church for years. Truculently they would declare that they had "no use for religion—of any kind"; that the "pious and their piety make me sick"; that they would "sooner be caught dead" than be "caught in church."

"It might be all right for those who need that kind of thing, but personally I could never take it very seriously," the prejudiced would often confess to the interviewer. Sometimes they would launch into the arguments they had had on the subject with friends, family, or minister. Frequently a significant turning point in their lives—and one reported with pride—was the time they "broke away from all that spiritual stuff" to devote themselves uninterruptedly to the practical aspects of life.

There were some prejudiced, however, who did go to church, even some who admitted that they attended quite regularly. But these people usually felt called upon to explain why they did, and their explanations always had something to do with conformity and nothing to do with inner conviction. Some went "to keep peace in the family," or "to show the children where they belonged." Some went to maintain their position in the community, or because they hoped that church membership might help them to achieve a better one. Some admitted unabashedly that they had joined a particular church "mostly for business reasons."

Whatever the story, it was evident that they used the church as they used all their other affiliations: for their own convenience, for their own advancement, and to bolster their own insecurity. Significantly, the only ones to refer to the Jews as "Christ-killers" were those who by their own admission believed in nothing, unless it was in the religion of Godless materialism.

It is understandable from all that we have discovered about him thus far that the highly prejudiced should be singularly unhappy about Jews and Judaism.

Since his hatred of Judaism is so often associated with his hatred of Christianity, he cannot see the one without being reminded of the other and the principles that govern both religions. It is to be expected that the concepts of justice, ethics, and the very idea of the brotherhood of all men would singularly unnerve the prejudiced.

It is also to be expected that one who flees in terror from all reflection, who believes that learning is harmful and deliberation useless except to freeze action, would find much to distress him in the tradition of learning that inheres in Judaism.

In Judaism's insistence upon the separation of man and

God and in the distinctions it draws between them, there is much to make the prejudiced shudder, because he often endows himself with more than human importance and authority, and frequently he confuses his leaders with God.

Finally, to one who is totally without faith in mankind because he is without faith in himself, the two-thousand-year survival of Jews cannot seem anything but a jeering reproach. For he knows nothing of the meaning of individual striving and he believes not at all in the ultimate triumph of justice and truth. He is governed by one rule only: "Vae Victis: Woe to the Conquered!" Under it he ranges his own destiny and that of his fellow-men. That the Jews should be alive at all today is an affront to all the rules the prejudiced person lives by; that any Jew should prosper is the most monstrous offense of all.

Among the ranks of the anti-Semites there can always be found some who are themselves Jewish, and they differ little from the others except that they tend to be more merciless in their denunciations.

The Jewish anti-Semite is usually determined to make the strongest possible attack upon other Jews, and since he faintly perceives that their economic or intellectual preoccupations may not be entirely deplorable in our American way of life, he generally concentrates his fire upon their "bad manners," their "ostentation," and their "social gaucherie." Sometimes he is hostile to no other group *but* Jews.

He shares with all the prejudiced, however, an abiding fear and dislike of himself. For he has been profoundly affected by the image of Jews so widely circulated by their enemies and he has come to think of himself precisely the way they think of him. Ceaselessly he scrutinizes his fellow-Jews for evidence of the traits ascribed to them, and when he finds some it is as though he were stabbed—as though he had found these also in himself.

But even as he privately associates himself with all Jews, publicly he insists upon severing himself from them. He appoints himself both judge and witness: as witness he testifies spiritedly to their sorry behavior and as judge he pronounces—but hopes to escape from—the punishment he considers their due.

Understandably his dream and his deepest desire is to achieve total assimilation—to be accepted as a man and to have his Jewishness forgotten—but the closer he draws to this dream the more wraithlike it seems to become. For if nothing else does, his own unremitting fears remind him constantly of his origins.

Nor can those Jews who do not wish to forget their Jewishness remain insensible to the wilderness of irrationality that surrounds them. Like the Negroes, they continue to nurse their vision of acceptance in an atmosphere that coolly continues to withhold it. Like their persecutors, they often mistake the results of prejudice for the causes of it and they try repeatedly to meet the attacks made upon them with reasoned arguments, with pertinent facts, and irrefutable evidence.

Some have cultivated impeccable "manners." Many impress upon their young the necessity for being "better than just good," because they are Jews. Others have deliberately sought employment in occupations Jews have been accused of shunning. Jewish organizations and individuals assume heavy responsibilities along with other groups, for furthering the health, welfare, and general security of all Americans.

But repeatedly they have made the disheartening discovery that if they are not condemned for one thing they will very likely be condemned for another—for it is in the nature of those who hate them to find something to justify their hatred, and if they cannot find it, then to invent it.

As the attacks upon them are often irrational, so too are the responses they elicit. Some Jews do behave precisely the way their tormentors say they do. Having discovered the futility of rational approaches and forthright appeals to gain the acceptance they so deeply desire, they may employ "shrewdness," or resort to "craftiness" and sometimes even to subterfuge. They may display too much zeal or too much defiance. They may brag too loudly about the achievements of one of their group or wither excessively because of the wrongdoings of another—all the while decrying those who would generalize unfairly about them.

If one is steadily persecuted one is quite likely to end up persecuting oneself, and unquestionably there are some Jews who behave as though they were responsible for their fate. Although their burden of guilt is not warranted they act just as though it might be, thus inciting to attack those who find in the cringing an irresistible prey. As Kipling's bleating kid incites the tiger, so the Jew's self-hatred not only invites but evokes, hatred from others.

Because their expectations are rooted in their memories, many Jews cannot easily rid themselves of the sense of more persecution to come. Therefore they may appear unduly apprehensive, impelled by a sense of imminent danger and the necessity to prepare for it even when no enemies are in sight.

More often, however, the Jews' response to injustice is to stiffen under it, for unlike the Negroes their memories are not of uninterrupted slavery but of miraculous survival. If they remember repeated persecutions, they remember much more forcefully the repeated defeats of their persecutors.

But no matter how well they behave they cannot affect fundamentally the feelings of those who are most prejudiced against them. For as those feelings were not caused by Jews they will not now be changed by them. Therefore the predicament of the Jew has been likened to that of the hero in one of Kafka's novels who is involved in a long trial, knowing neither his judge nor his jury, nor even what he is being tried for—knowing only that he is considered guilty. Although the judgment is constantly postponed and he profits from these delays to find a thousand safeguards for himself, with each new precaution he takes he comes to believe increasingly in his guilt. Though his circumstances may appear promising from the outside (for while decision is withheld freedom is still possible) the indeterminate trial tears at him invisibly. For it cannot be otherwise.

It is, then, much as John Hersey described it to be when he spoke of the wall that exists between Jews and Gentiles. The actual masonry is often done by the Jews, but it is the Gentiles who ask that the wall be built and who, to insure its effectiveness, design the blueprints, provide the materials for it, and at times even help in its construction.

But whether it is a "place" we design for some of our fellow-men or a "wall" we build against some others—fear remains the architect.

6

The Super-Patriot
and the Anti-Patriot

We have seen the extremes to which some people will go to avoid the discovery of their own shortcomings. We have seen, for example, how they will cling to the flimsiest of evidence to prove that Jews, Negroes, foreigners, bureaucrats, anyone and everyone but themselves, are responsible for their difficulties.

Like migratory birds they seem to change their hates as if these were plumage, to fit the season and the surroundings. Because they are more conventional than consistent they would even shed a prejudice or two rather than seem monstrous in the public eye. In fact, if it were to become fashionable to defend those whom they most disliked, their voices would likely be heard among all the other voices calling for tolerance, equality, and whatever else "the best people" happened to be calling for at the moment.

But although in the opinions they express such people may seem changeable as the seasons, the way in which they view events as well as people remains remarkably constant. Wherever their eyes light they see defects and deficiencies and all appear unwarrantably of the same dimensions and significance. They seem to look upon the world in much the same way as a wrecking crew looks upon a shaky super-structure: they can see in it only raw materials for the junk heap.

It should not surprise us, therefore, to find that though the prejudiced may limber up on minority groups it is in the playground of politics that he really stretches his limbs. Here in the dress of a wide-awake citizen he can deplore and decry to his heart's content. Here, assuming the posture of a devoted patriot—and in the company of the most respected patriots—he can assiduously expose all of society's weak spots, thereby diverting attention from his own.

Throughout the *Studies* many links were noticeable between politics and prejudice, although some of the most significant ones were rather implicit in the data than explicit in the findings.

There was the connection between prejudice and conservatism, for example. Earlier investigations had turned up some evidence to suggest that the highly prejudiced was more likely to espouse the conservative than the liberal viewpoint on political and economic matters. The explanation offered for this was that his deep-lying pessimism combined with his lack of faith in humankind appeared to make him an ardent supporter of the *status quo* and a strong opponent of all social and economic innovations.

The scientists were anxious to discover whether this alleged relationship actually existed, and they attempted therefore to measure the conservatism or the liberalism of an equal number of those who had scored "high" and those who had scored "low" on the questionnaires having to do with minority group prejudice. Their data, however, yielded no definitive conclusions, for while many of the highly prejudiced were of conservative persuasion, some were not. And while most of those low in prejudice appeared to support the liberal viewpoint, a number were also to be found defending the conservative position.

As a matter of fact, it was not the *substance* but the *rigidity* of their beliefs that distinguished the highly prejudiced from most of those low in prejudice. Whether they favored unions or opposed them; whether they urged more free enterprise or none at all, whether they spoke for social change or against it, the prejudiced stated their positions unconditionally. They could neither admit nor imagine any other position but their own.

In their discussions of political issues, however, a few of the "lows" revealed personality traits closely resembling those of the "highs." Although they appeared to have almost a standard position of "tolerance" toward minority groups (which accounted for their low scores on those questionnaires), they were apt to be dogmatic about all their opinions. They appeared full of resentment toward any number of things and people and they attacked ruthlessly numerous groups, other than racial and religious, to which they did not belong, such as "big business," "management," "politicians," etc.

When these authoritarians—"highs" or "lows"—discussed public issues, they rarely spoke of the principles that pertained to them; they always spoke of the dangers implicit in them. They rarely spoke of values; they always spoke of costs. When they discussed trade unions, for example, they would speak of the threat unions could (or should) be to industry; when they talked of taxes they would speak of their burden; when they talked of public education they would speak of its costs.

No matter what they talked about they would criticise more than they would praise, they would punish more than they would reward and, of course, they would wreck more than they would preserve. When they talked about the government, for example, they could speak only of the foibles of the bureaucrats; when they discussed political parties, they would talk mainly about their corruption; when they spoke of the possibilities of peace, they could imagine only the possible uses of power.

Whether he used the language of the conservative or that of the liberal, it was quite evident that when the authoritarian stated his views concerning any public issue, he was simultaneously recording his philosophy of life. For he proceeded on the assumption that the world was lost and whirling, strayed as in the night from all its earlier paths of decency and goodness, doomed by the darkness to a hopeless struggle with evil that was as universal as it was invisible.

In all of his interviews and in every phase of the investigations, it was clear that the authoritarian thought of his citizen-functions in terms of his role in such a struggle, for he seemed to measure his patriotism by the number of dangers he could identify and attack. Similarly, he would judge the patriotism of others not by the confidence they expressed in —or truly felt about—their country, but by the evil they could discover within its boundaries. In his conversations with the interviewers, he would miss no opportunity to tell of unrest and discontent throughout the land. He would relate in liveliest detail stories of confusion among public officials, deceitfulness among elected representatives, ignorance among the leaders of our own and other countries. He would offer this information as if it were a contribution, savoring its tragedy as if it were a comedy.

In striking contrast were the attitudes recorded during interviews with most of those low in prejudice, the non-authoritarians. Much more often than not, their starting point was their faith in their country and their profound commitment to democracy. Whether they explained this faith and this commitment in terms of their liberalism or their conservatism, they reasoned that the best way to protect democracy was to practice it, not to demolish it. And this was the reasoning they brought to whatever issues they discussed.

They would not categorically accept or reject the notion of government controls, for example, simply because their party would or would not be doing the controlling. They would accept some controls if they thought these would further individual security; otherwise they would reject them.

They would not urge increased taxation in order to punish the well-to-do, nor would they oppose it because they were "tired of pouring their hard-earned money down the drain." They would support additional taxation if they approved the purpose for which it was required; otherwise they would oppose it.

They would not urge the strengthening of unions in order to "put industry in its place"; or the strengthening of industry so as to "tell unions where to get off." More often they would recommend a balance of power between the two, and responsibility shared by both.

Naturally, they differed greatly among themselves in the

opinions they offered. Some were cautious, others more adventurous in their solutions. As they would elect different routes they would also travel at different rates of speed. But the goal toward which they traveled was one and the same. Conservative or liberal, they sought protection for the individual not suppression of him, an extension of freedom not a diminution of it. When they expressed any fear—and they often did—it was a fear *for* democracy and not *because* of it.

In the presence of those who hold such views, the highly prejudiced can feel only acute discomfort. They might echo their words if it should prove advantageous to do so; they might even borrow their doctrines; but the prejudiced cannot possibly borrow the moderation that characterized them or the faith that framed them. For their fears have made such individuals addicts of extremism. In the realm of politics the drugs they require are excessive credence or excessive doubt: they can live on either but not without one or the other.

The authoritarians, then, must live not among the patriots —the bona fide conservatives or the true liberals—but among the super-patriots or the anti-patriots. There, no one will criticize them for their hates or ridicule them for their fears; they may even be rewarded for them and certainly they will be encouraged in them. In the province of either the reactionaries or the revolutionaries, they can live in great comfort. For in either place such individuals can find the kind of joy and hope that means so much to them—the joy of being a slave and the hope of being a master.

It may have been the first time Americans heard the warning, for it was in 1787 at the time of the Constitutional Convention: "When a people shall become incapable of governing themselves and fit for a master," said George Washington, "it is of little consequence from what quarter he comes."

Today there are few among us who do not clearly perceive this. Communists and fascists alike are properly damned for their truculence, their deceptions, and above all their arrant disregard for the dignity and the rights of human beings. Events have starkly exposed the similarity of their goals as well as their methods: the goal of both being the seizure of power, their method the suppression of the individual. From the standpoint of our country's safety it is hardly important whether people who are bent on destruction choose the catapult of the revolutionaries or the fortresses of the reactionaries from which to execute their demolition: "the madness is equal" and so too is the danger.

In the years prior to and immediately following World War II, however, the resemblance between the extreme left and the extreme right was not so discernible. In those days there seemed to many to be a vast difference between the promise held by each. That they filled different needs for the individuals who were drawn to them is quite evident in the many recent retrospective studies of the character of the Communist and fascist movements in this country during that period.

One such study, *Appeals of Communism*, by Gabriel A. Almonde, published in 1954 by the Princeton University Press, provides impressive confirmation of that which is now well known to informed students of the subject, namely, that the individuals in this country who were most attracted to Communist doctrine in the years prior to World War II were not so much persuaded as they were satisfied by it. What appears to have satisfied them most was the opportunity it offered to conspire in secret against society, in company with others whose private misery was as great as or greater than their own.

These were individuals bedeviled not so much by the practical problems of life as by the emotional ones. Unlike those in other countries who were drawn to the Communist Party, the rank and file members in the United States were frequently well educated and almost never poverty stricken. But they were men and women who according to their own testimony had always felt "left out of things": they were socially ill at ease, sometimes weak physically. Often they told of parents who had either overawed them or neglected them. In their *Report on the American Communist,* published in 1952, Morris Ernst and David Loth were struck particularly by "the extremely high incidence of suicides, desertions, and divorces among the parents, brothers and sisters, or other close relatives of Communists."

In short, these were people who were dissatisfied with themselves and with society, but they preferred to reverse the order of their dissatisfactions. They found it easier to justify a revolution against institutions that seemingly had failed so many than a rebellion against the family that had failed them alone. Though they were often from churchgoing families and frequently from middle-class homes, most severed their relationships with home and church at the time they joined the Communists. These, they explained, seemed too rigid to reflect a world they were convinced was exploding around them. The planet, not they, seemed to be reeling; established institutions, not they, seemed to be straining and breaking at the seams.

They generally reported that at the outset they had given the Party all their ardor, and for a while it had satisfied them. There was the relief of expressing the rebellion surging within them. There was the excitement of finding constant camaraderie after years of intense loneliness. There was the wonder of feeling useful, of belonging somewhere, to something.

But the seduction soon lost its hold—for some sooner than for others. Morris Ernst and David Loth reported that the majority of the rank and file had not only joined but had left the Party by the time they were twenty-three years old. Some rather quickly discovered that though they were surrounded by comrades they were still without friends. They found that although they loved the masses unreservedly the feeling was not reciprocated, and the relationship therefore was anything but satisfying. Some found what they were looking for outside of the Party (namely, love, acceptance, or recognition for themselves—not for the proletariat) and the moment they did they left their fellow-revolutionaries without delay and without regret.

For others the break was longer in coming and harder to achieve. They clung steadfastly to the Party until they could no longer stretch their explanations to defend the treachery they witnessed within it. They left then not in relief but in desperation, and suffering greater anguish than that which had driven them to the Party in the first place. For they had come to it hungry for a faith and anxious to prove themselves by their dedication. Now they were once again without something to believe in—and far from proving themselves they had disgraced themselves.

These later studies also report that former Communists

rarely seem to change in personality as a result of their experience with communism. Those who were ruthless, or bitter, or timid, or anxious to dodge the difficult task of making their own decisions, seem to remain that way. So do those who were gentle or thoughtful or anxious or unhappy. Some seek out other causes in which to lose themselves.

Some, in a frenzied effort to regain both faith and face, assume the role of super-patriot and play it with the same feverish intensity that characterized their earlier performance as an anti-patriot. Once they believed that all who refused to betray their country were either dupes of the capitalists or incredibly naïve. Now they believe that all who refuse to join them in their denunciations or who disagree with them in any way are either dupes of the Communists, or incredibly naïve.

But even in their new role of super-patriot they continue to think of their citizen responsibilities in strictly lethal terms: they must attack and expose, not themselves but others who once were caught up by the Communist fervor. Moreover, by showing how strong and influential that movement once was they hope to make more palatable to themselves and to everyone else their own earlier surrender to it. They are, however, repudiating only the cause to which they once surrendered; they do not—because they cannot—question the surrender itself. For the same need overpowers them still, the need for "selfless" dedication to something they can believe in unquestioningly. Only by burying *themselves* are these super-patriots (formerly anti-patriots) able to bury their fears.

Such is the tragedy of their natures that their new-found cause of Americanism cannot possibly hold them for long.

For they lack so completely the essential element of the democratic personality, namely, faith in oneself and in one's fellow-man. These are people far better suited to martyr themselves in a spurious defense of their country than they are to live according to its principles and its creeds.

These later investigations also help to explain the nature of the attraction the extreme right might hold for the highly prejudiced. There, in the province of reaction, are people also without hope, and many without conscience as well. Theirs does not seem to be a need for selfless dedication, but for selfish opportunism. They too are convinced that the world is in shipwreck but *they* are determined to survive. And their formula for survival is to throw overboard as many others as possible.

The reactionary does not seek a cause in which he may lose himself; he seeks an opportunity to express himself and to express particularly all the anger and resentment within him. The Communist may have needed a faith more than he needed a revolution, but the reactionary needs *action* more than he needs *dedication*.

On the evidence offered by many of these studies, one might conclude that while the rank and file Communist is full of resentment and even hatred of many things and people in the world around him, racial and religious prejudices are likely to be incidental to his mental outlook. The presence or absence of such prejudice is likely to reflect "official policy" of the Party rather than his own convictions. He will act on the matter of prejudice precisely as he acts on all other issues: just as the Party instructs him to act. He will exploit minorities if it conforms to Party purpose and he will refrain from doing so if it does not. The inviolability of the individual has no meaning for him whatsoever.

The reactionary, however, is not likely to be found without such prejudices, for these are integral to his personality, inherent in his philosophy. Once the prejudiced joins the province of the reactionaries, therefore, he is not apt to desert it. For he is easily satisfied by their racist appeals, by the occasional demonstrations of violence he finds there, and particularly by the promises of more violence to come. In dreams of destruction he finds infinite solace.

Patriotism is also the anodyne the reactionary uses. Tirelessly he will whip up and mix up real and imaginary dangers to his country in order to support his pessimism and to justify the power and the violence he yearns for. He may claim that he "chokes up with emotion" when he hears "The Star-Spangled Banner." He may insist that "any one of our boys can lick ten from any country you name." He may declare that "no country can hold a candle to America." But though he sings his country's praises loudly, he sings louder still of the troubles she is in, due in the main to "radicals," to "foreign agitators," to Negroes, to Jews. Before long his great faith in his country turns out to be no faith at all. For when he talks but a moment or two longer it becomes manifest that the only thing of which he is really certain is the imminence of her doom.

In the world of politics this is the company the authoritarian personality keeps. Knowing the secret of his character, namely the boundless terror he carries within him, we might expect to find him here. Super-patriot, anti-patriot, reactionary, or revolutionary—ironically they are nurtured chiefly by one another. When the Communist speaks, the reactionary is confirmed in his calling; when the reactionary acts up, the Communist could ask no finer confirmation of his own dismal prophecies. Each finds in the other ultimate justification for his own excesses. Collectively, they comprise a large proportion of the fear-ridden of the nation.

Happily, many of us are not that fearful. Authorities who claim to be all-knowing and all-mighty are not what we are searching for. We are more worried than reassured by the spectre of great concentrations of power. We have no desire either to wield it or to worship it. Given a choice of a large measure of freedom or a large measure of authority, most of us would not hesitate more than a moment before we chose freedom.

Yet the voices of the relatively few very fearful—those of the super-patriots and the anti-patriots—are clearly heard in our land today. To be sure, their very brashness commands attention for it is often impossible to ignore their impudence. In order to display their courage they regularly demonstrate their callousness. To prove their power they make a constant show of their inhumanity. To establish their own rectitude they are incessantly seeing falseness in others. No head is too sacred to fall, no office taboo for their attacks.

Theirs are also the least uncertain of all the voices heard today, for they are quick to cut the cloth of the universe to fit the meagre dimensions of their own understanding. In a jiffy they turn world-sized problems into country-sized ones and giant-sized complexities into pygmy-sized simplicities.

Rhetoric, in fact, is their chief weapon. It is they who have endowed our decade with a whole new glossary of terms that breathe contempt for mankind. Their spokesmen are masters at echoing the fears of their listeners and more masterful still at explaining them in ways that will keep their pride intact. In their endless recitations of the trouble we are in, they try to include something for everyone: "not we the patriots, they the treasonous, are the cause of our difficulties"; "not we the native born, they the foreign born"; "not we the taxpayers, they the bureaucrats"; "not we the parents, they the teachers"; "not we the voters, they the politicians"; "not we the people, it the government. . . ."

Radical or reactionary, their arguments reach people who are of neither persuasion. The malice of their message is spread by the gossip of those who hardly believe it but are somehow curiously influenced by it. Substantial citizens who start out by insisting they cannot agree with a word of what they hear, after a while confess that they must agree with some of it, and end up by agreeing with more than they ever thought they could.

Steadily they feed their listeners' virtuous indignation. Skillfully they tap the vein of fear that runs through the heart of America and the world today. For all around us are tensions and conflicts that might well strain idealism to the point of reaction and optimism to the point of collapse. In our time it is easy to confuse reasonable and unreasonable grounds for fear, and it is easier still to mistake the sound of pessimism for the sound of wisdom.

"Love renders its votaries credulous," an ancient seer observed. Neither the super-patriot nor the anti-patriot is apt to know much about love, but he knows all there is to know about fear and he counts on it to work in much the same way. He asks only that people listen to him. For he has reason to believe that if they will heed his catastrophic prophecies, they will also heed his remedy. If they agree with his estimate of the menace, they must come ultimately to agree with his estimate of the power necessary to subdue it.

The super-patriot may come from the province of today's reactionaries or yesterday's revolutionaries. The anti-patriot may come from the ranks of the revolutionaries—yesterday's or today's. Whatever the province from which they currently speak, they are understandably eager for recruits from other provinces and they are marvellously indifferent to the labels their followers attach to themselves. They receive with equal joy those who call themselves conservatives, those who call themselves liberals, and those who are too confused or too frightened to call themselves anything at all.

The recruits, for their part, can be equally indifferent to the loyalties they profess, for once they have joined the ranks of the authoritarians it is of little consequence in which regiments they march. Their leaders are of one mind and their separate efforts—should they continue unimpeded—can have but a single result: the establishment in these United States of a government of the fearful, by the fearful, and for the fearful.

Part Three

The
Reduction
of
Fear

———

7

Accept the Unalterable

> The search for Truth is in one way hard and
> in another easy. For it is evident that no one
> can master it fully nor miss it wholly. But
> each adds a little to our knowledge of Nature,
> and from all the facts assembled there arises a
> certain grandeur.
>
> —ARISTOTLE

Having traveled with the experts through their separate
realms of social and psychological theories, we have come
upon surprisingly many areas of common ground as to the
origins and consequences of prejudice.

There is agreement that from the cradle to the grave we are
encouraged in our prejudices and that these grow as the child
grows and flourish in the minds of men as long as their surroundings provoke them and their environment stimulates
them.

There is agreement that intensely prejudiced people are
angry people, having issued from a childhood where hope
was unavailing and pain unending. They are people who
could not—and still cannot—frankly criticize mother's
failures and father's foibles; instead, they pronounce stern

103

judgment on all the rest of the world and nurse a permanent grievance against most of the people in it.

But the prejudiced are also fearful and they are not likely to express their prejudices unless popular belief confirms them—or unless they are sure it is "safe" to do so. Therefore they will lash out at those who are weaker than they are or at those whom a great many other people appear also to dislike.

Finally, there is agreement that the victims of prejudice have little to do with the cause of it. They are likely to be people whom a tragic combination of circumstances has rendered both accessible and vulnerable and therefore eminently suited for victimization by those casting around for someone on whom to unleash the full force of their fears.

The task now at hand is the reduction of prejudice—not decades from now but in our own generation; not only in those who are young and still growing, but among those now fully grown; not only in the people around us, but even in ourselves. We know now that the roots of prejudice run deep. By adulthood they are for the most part inaccessible. This is not true of its offshoots, however, and like weeds in a lovely or useful garden, the offshoots of prejudice must be attacked without too much consideration for their origins.

If we are to apply our new knowledge to the execution of this task then we shall need, in the words of the familiar trilogy, the strength to endure that which we may be unable to change, the courage to change what we can, and the wisdom to know the difference.

At the outset we must accept a hard set of facts concerning the world, our country, and ourselves. Few of these, however, are immutable. Most, in fact, are amenable to change.

"All parts of the world are simultaneously out of joint," wrote David Cohn recently. "The commonwealth of fear is universal." In the history of mankind fear has often been known to mother insight, to rouse men from their lethargy and cause them to heed dangers they might otherwise have overlooked. But that is not happening to many of us today, for although the reasons for some fears are indeed rational, our responses to them are not.

The shrillest alarms today are sounded by those who as shrilly insist that we can do nothing to save ourselves. Chronic pessimists, seemingly glad to find further reasons for their own pessimism, warn of the growing power of our enemies and predict disaster for all who may be unfortunate enough to tangle with them. At the same time, however, they oppose all cooperative efforts to prevent such a tangle. None of these, they argue, is strong enough or powerful enough to deal successfully with such mighty antagonists as we now have. In short, they bring to the world scene no more hope than they bring to their personal lives—and their attitudes toward both attest not to their confidence in men but only to their contempt for them.

Many of us, on the other hand, find no comfort in the idea of society in shipwreck and we cannot make ourselves believe that there is no escape from our present distress. But for the most part we remain silent and detached, almost as though we deliberately chose to view the major problems in the world through the wrong end of a telescope so that they might seem tiny and remote. Either because we cannot bear to think of the enormity of the danger or because we feel so helpless in the face of it, we busy ourselves attacking and criticising one another rather than attending to the things that imperil us all.

In addition to the fear-laden atmosphere that embraces so much of the world, there are many special elements in our American atmosphere to spur our antipathies toward one another. Earlier we noted the inescapable dilemma of a people confronted with a profoundly impelling creed and equally impelling reasons to forget it. Prejudice and inequities are most doggedly defended in the name of individual freedom. Individual freedom, it is often declared, must include the freedom to hate, to exclude, and to discriminate.

The *right* to become a smashing success is interpreted as an *obligation* to become one, and ethics and ideals are generally strained through the sieve of practicality. Throughout the *Studies,* notions of brotherhood and fair play were greeted partly with incredulity and partly with scorn, as one after another told of the ruins of their youthful idealism—tumbled hither and thither in the strenuous pursuit of their dreams.

For a surprisingly large number Horatio Alger still called the tune, and though his image appeared more taunting than inspiring to the prejudiced, it continued to throb in their imaginations. The contrast between the promise Horatio personified and the reality that confronted them was more than most could endure without great anger. All during their interviews, intent upon explaining and defending their own limitations, "*he* is at fault—not I" was the chant they monotonously intoned. Noteworthy too were the number of accusations they could pursue simultaneously, their anger toward one rarely extinguishing or diminishing their anger toward another.

But although there was often a random quality about their vituperation, it settled most confidently upon those who were least like themselves. For the ones who were "different" their sympathy was coldest, and the "different," therefore, bore the brunt of the profound disappointment the prejudiced felt in themselves.

Most of us, as far back as we can remember, heard with pride of the epic past of our country. We learned that she was a land made glorious and mighty by the blending of many cultures and nationalities; that she was a country where differences were merged and dissolved by the miraculous solvent known as freedom; that it was this fact more than any other that bestowed upon our land its unique vitality.

Throughout the *Studies,* however, this notion seemed alive with irony. For where there were differences there was fear and, inevitably, hostility. Moreover, while there appeared to be an acute fear of those who were *obviously* different, there was also a chronic and gnawing fear of those who *might* be different but who could not readily be identified as such: the light Negro "who could easily pass," the Jew "who looked like everyone else," the next-door neighbor of same faith and skin who, because he "buried himself in books," seemed "strangely different from the rest of us."

In a country teeming with differences, this nameless and pervasive fear of those who are different is among the most challenging and disturbing of the *Studies'* disclosures.

The utilitarian strain in our society has other unhappy effects on us. A striking number of those interviewed appeared quite innocent of reflection: their opinions were virtually confined to the values of work, the dangers of play, and the futility of love. Their dreams were of the simplest kind: inheriting an easy fortune, telling a captious boss where to go, seeing a son or a husband become "something important." "Puttering around" was the leisure-time activity listed by many of the men; "socializing" by many of the women— for this, they would often explain, was probably the best way of climbing into society more interesting or more impressive than their present one.

Many confessed to a recurrent and sometimes to a persistent sense of loneliness, to feelings of futility about themselves and all of their enterprises. A surprising number of the veterans, for example, admitted a reluctance to leave the army at war's end, for there they had known purposefulness and companionship not experienced before or since army days. Parents often dwelled upon their hope that their children would "know where they belonged," would "find a place for themselves" and "know enough to stay in it, once they found it."

Here, as in so many instances, the difference between the highly prejudiced and those low in prejudice was a matter of degree. When we are lonely many of us tend to wedge ourselves more tightly than ever into our surroundings. But this is especially true of the highly prejudiced. Their conversations were more often studded with complaints about "not belonging" and "nobody really caring one way or the other" what happened to them. For them admission to the crowd is tantamount to admission to a fortress when the guns are going off.

In a society where crown-mindedness is considered laudatory, and conformity is looked upon as the order of the day, such individuals and their hostilities find utmost encouragement and support.

Nor are the *best* civilized among us necessarily the *most* civilized or the most humane. For it is possible to do most of the things our civilization requires of us and still not view the world or ourselves with benevolence. In the *Studies*, for example, were many who had *been* good but who somehow had failed to *make* good. All around them they saw evidence of those with far less goodness enjoying far greater rewards. "Perhaps virtue is not its own reward after all," the world seemed to be hinting; perhaps, they thought, there is more to life than the maxim-mongers would have them believe. Smarting inwardly at the way the world has cheated them, these people were filled with hatreds: many petty, some intense, many simmering, some smouldering.

There were also those who had *made* good but in the process had neglected to *be* good. Consequently they often felt sure that their prosperity was more fortunate than deserved. They stood behind their success almost stealthily, guarding it fearfully lest the same kind of accident that brought it return one day and whisk it away.

There were even some who had been good *and* made good but they were likely to be so worn out by the struggle attending their achievement that what little sympathy they could muster they reserved strictly for themselves.

In the light of all this, the temptation becomes great to place at society's doorstep full responsibility for the malevolence within it. It is easy to exclaim (because it is to some extent true) that the world as it is today encourages and even breeds anger, that it provides fertile ground for a host of fears and a comparable number of hates. As we elbow our way to our desires, there is little to promote magnanimity toward one another. There is every reason to want to hold some people down, to keep some back, and to find acceptable reasons for doing both.

But we are the creators as much as we are the victims of our environment, and the moral acrobatics we perform in the course of our daily dealings with one another reflect our individual vagrancy quite as much as society's. Among the more disquieting facts we must accept, therefore, is that there are many adults among us who, because of afflictions of mind and spirit suffered years ago, have achieved a skeptical stability at best.

It was startling to see how often the anger expressed by a prejudiced adult turned out to be nearly as old as he was himself. Usually he had acquired it in the first years of his life when he was forced to learn the most difficult lessons life has to teach long before he could understand them. He had learned too early, for example, that instincts are not always for expression, that love is not necessarily reciprocal, that promises are not always fulfilled, nor punishments always just. Usually these were the *first* things he had learned, and since he had no other reassuring experiences to cushion him against the shock of their discovery, they had served for him as a lasting introduction to the ways of the world.

Small wonder that as adults such people should devote themselves to chastising the world rather than to living in it— and that no matter what it is they speak of, they speak in accents of anger! Asked their opinions, they will offer their doubts; asked their experiences, they will tell of their disappointments; asked about their friends, they will talk about their enemies.

Such people are capable of the most intense and damaging hatred upon the slightest provocation, and there may be little if anything we can do to help them. But while they, like storms in nature, play themselves out, we can certainly protect ourselves from their wanton assaults.

There are others, a shade less destructive perhaps, who for reasons also rooted in childhood have a talent for worrying, a genius for finding things to worry about and people to blame for their anxieties. To hear them describe the universe they inhabit is to wonder how they managed to survive so cruel and heartless a world. Commonplace setbacks seem to them major catastrophes; the slightest stings feel to them like mortal wounds. There may not be a great deal we can do to change these people either, for they are destined, in the words of Antisthenes, to be "devoured by their own disposition as iron is by rust." Before they are, however, we must realize that they will probably try to devour a great many others. But again, we must prevent them from doing so.

Finally, we must accept the fact that those who are most prejudiced are the last to admit that fact, or even to recognize it. They produce endless arguments to prove the reasonableness of their hostility and they hear no evidence that might disprove their contentions. There is no end to the tricks their eyes and ears perform so that they may see only those things they wish to see and hear only those things they wish to hear.

These are usually people with overdeveloped fears and underdeveloped consciences—and these two conditions sustain them as they hurl endless and unwarranted accusations at those around them. They do not mean to lie about others; they mean only to keep from knowing the facts about themselves. Fugitives from themselves and therefore from the truth, their determination to avoid the truth renders the prejudiced all but anesthetic to it.

This, then, is one aspect of our present terrain—unquestionably a formidable one. The real question, however, is whether the land and its inclinations, and the people and their tendencies, are really as devastated as they seem. There is a great deal to suggest that they are not, that in our conscientious study of the shadows we have simply had our backs to the sun. We must turn toward it now, if we are to have a total and therefore a true picture of our environment.

8

Change the Changeable

> The essence of knowledge is, having it, to apply it; not having it, to confess your ignorance.
>
> —CONFUCIUS

Our university laboratories and libraries are bursting with discoveries that promise much for humanity. But only a fraction of them seem to find their way into everyday life.

Practical men offer many explanations for this state of affairs. They argue that the scientists have a language all their own, so remote from the common speech of the nation as to be almost a dialect. They maintain that it is one thing to offer huge structures of theory and doctrine and quite another to reshape the world in accordance with them. The statistical-minded warn of the dangers of applying data gained from the study of scant thousands, to the problems of hundreds of millions. The conservative-minded hint at the impropriety of drawing bold conclusions from observations offered tentatively at best.

Such warnings are well-taken as, indeed, such criticism is often well-founded. For while these new insights into human behavior open many vistas for the solution of our

113

problems, they do not lessen the complexity of them. Rival practitioners, in fact, may (and often do) draw from these insights very different prescriptions for achieving human betterment.

Such rivalries and disputes, however, are certain to recede as the lines of communications are opened, and are kept open, between those who are studying human behavior and those who without always knowing much about it are responsible for shaping and influencing it. With what we now know we are far from being able to reshape the world. We are close, however, to being able to set realistic goals for ourselves and to select the methods most likely to achieve them. As we thus stabilize our expectations, automatically we increase our chances of fulfilling them.

"Train up a child in the way he should go: and when he is older he will not depart from it." So it is stated in the Book of Proverbs; and so it is also stated in the *Studies* which illumine, perhaps more than they extend, ancient wisdom. In their insistent correlations between adult character and childhood experience, however, are findings of considerable contemporary importance. These point to the great need for expanding parent education programs which will be attentive not only to the details of child-raising but to the principles of it as well. For although these principles are by now well known to students of human behavior, they are little known and even less understood by those who have the job of raising children, not of studying them.

There was the tie, for example, between warmth and affection received during childhood and the quality of optimism and friendliness that shows itself in later years. It was

vividly demonstrated that those who had experienced sympathy and understanding when they were young are much
more able to offer it to others now, as adults. To have been
loved is to know how to love; and to love and be loved is to
be hopeful about life and most of the people one meets during the course of it.

Those adults most understanding of shortcomings in
others usually recalled that as children their mistakes had
been sympathetically attributed to an immaturity they could
not help, rather than to wilful misbehavior. Those now most
considerate of the rights of others generally remembered
that as children they had been treated "like human beings":
they had been allowed to express their opinions, if not
always to act in accordance with them, and in this way they
had come to value freedom of expression for themselves and
for others too.

On the other hand the memories of the intolerant bristled
with tales of punishments as bruising as they were bewildering; and these memories appeared to be the stimuli for their
bruising of others, years later, in a manner comparably harsh
and arbitrary. These people would recall how "father's word
was law," or that "we kids wouldn't have dared to question
decisions that were handed down to us," and in telling these
tales they seemed to be illustrating principles that guided
them still. For even now as adults they carried with them the
old fear and foreboding associated with opinions that differed
from the "accepted" ones; even now they believed that
those who dared to express them not only invited, but deserved, the most severe castigation.

Then there were the adults who were constantly advocating "restrictions" to ensure that some people "stayed where

they belonged." With astonishing consistency these men and women would tell of a childhood in which there had been either the most severe restraints imposed or absolutely none at all!

Those who had been curbed too often and too much—those who were always made to feel "too young," "too small," too ignorant, or too incompetent to do the things they had wanted to do—had little or no opportunity to discover their true capacities. On the other hand, those who had known no restrictions were repeatedly attempting things they could not possibly achieve, only to experience one disaster after another. When, for example, a child is permitted to dive into deep water before he has learned to swim, or allowed to crawl up a steep flight of steps before he has learned to walk, these experiences can only impress him cruelly with his weakness and give him much more reason for fear than for confidence in himself.

It is understandable that boundaries—even the most arbitrary ones—should seem essential to those who had never learned to live without them. It is equally understandable that those who did not have them when they so much needed them should now eagerly invite them. All these individuals will always insist—as they insisted in the *Studies*—that the boundaries they advocate are to keep others in their place; but the truth is, that the curbs they seek are not for "others" at all, but only for themselves. The restrictions they impose upon others are their protection from their own real or imagined weakness.

In contrast were those who had grown up knowing the comfort of reasonable authority, and boundaries at once protective enough and flexible enough to permit them to test their emerging strength and to discover their limitations simultaneously without undue pain or shock. These were the men and women who now seemed to have outgrown the need for restrictions, finding most of them unwarrantably confining and superfluous.

It will be remembered how anxious were the parents of the most prejudiced youngsters to have their children "toe the mark" and behave "as well as any child their age." Parents of the unprejudiced children were far more concerned with the individual qualities and aptitudes of their young. Their children's uniqueness, not their "normality," was of paramount interest to them. It is not surprising, therefore, that the child whose own needs have been answered, whose individuality has been deftly captured and eagerly developed, should respond cheerfully to the variety of interests and needs in those around him. It is also not surprising that the child who has been trained to behave as much like "everyone else" as he possibly can, will react with fear and trembling whenever he finds himself in the presence of those who are different from "everyone else."

But all these lessons in the area of parent-child relationships are reducible to a single lesson, namely, that sympathy, understanding, acceptance of oneself and therefore of others must be learned in childhood if they are to become permanent character traits. *They can be learned there, however, only if they are experienced there.* Sometimes, to be sure, they are acquired later in life and belatedly tacked on to one's personality. But then they are worn almost as ornaments, and like ornaments their use is dictated by fashion and convenience—either one being sufficient reason to order their discard.

If all parents were to learn and to apply this lesson to the upbringing of their young, we would soon begin to see a considerable reduction in prejudice among those who are now young, among those who are still growing, and eventually, of course, among those who are fully grown. But the best and the worst that can be said for parents is that they are only human; and of those who might hear about these findings there will be many who, because of their own earlier scars or later unhappiness, will be untouched by them.

There will be others who may appreciate the findings but be unable to apply them. Knowing the importance of a serene and happy family life will not help perpetually harassed parents to achieve it. Knowing her child's hunger for love will not make a loveless mother able to provide it. Knowing that emotional needs unfilled in childhood can probably not be filled at all will not help an insensitive parent either to recognize those needs or to fill them.

Then too it is the job of parents to train their children to live in the world, not to hide from it, and they cannot do this if they establish and maintain values that are too precious for everyday use. They must try, of course, to create an atmosphere at home that is more protective and more satisfying than the world outside—but it cannot be too much so, for then all they may succeed in doing is to contribute to society one or several members ill-prepared for its travail and destined, therefore, to hate it.

If parent education were to take hold, it could well become a most dependable and lasting cure for prejudice, for this would be attacking prejudice at its roots. But inasmuch as parents are not always educable, and inasmuch as the home cannot become a great deal better than the society in which it resides, we cannot count too heavily upon this approach to achieve a significant reduction in prejudice in the near future. Furthermore, since we are not to be allowed to wait around for generations to observe our progress, a variety of other efforts must proceed simultaneously.

Moreover, these must proceed on the assumption that the hostility now here is here to stay—and that more is doubtless in the making. It is quite possible, however, to discourage and even to prohibit the most damaging expressions of it, to capture and route much of this free-floating anger so that it spends itself on those humans who are responsible for it instead of on those who are not.

Whenever Americans feel discouraged about any of the ills that afflict their society, they are likely to suggest that education is one or even the only answer. The vaguer they are as to its content, the more enthusiastic they are apt to become about their remedy. In the *Studies* the most prejudiced individuals prescribed it regularly, cautioning as they did so that none of us would live to see its influence.

Parents of the most hostile youngsters would stoutly maintain that it was "up to the schools to teach tolerance." It was obvious, however, that they did not take their proposal seriously. For the very ones who were most eager to pass this particular buck to the schools were the first to object most strenuously, in another context, to the schools' acceptance of it. Whenever they were asked their opinion of what the schools should teach they would assert the supreme importance of the 3 R's and "practical training," and they would characterize angrily all social studies and similar courses as "unnecessary frills" or a "useless extravagance."

As a matter of fact, under the system of education that prevails in great sections of our country, it would seem quite possible to spend many years in a variety of schools and universities acquiring sundry degrees and diplomas, and to emerge from all of it with one's prejudices intact—perhaps, though, with a greater facility for defending them. In the *Studies* highly prejudiced individuals were evident among university students as well as among those who had barely a grammar school education; and individuals low in prejudice were likely to turn up among those without much formal education as well as among those who had completed graduate studies.

Consideration and respect for others is not something that can be either learned or taught like the multiplication table. Nevertheless, the schools can help greatly in the cultivation of such attitudes. The extent to which they do so depends not alone on what they teach but also on the atmosphere in which the teaching takes place and, of course, on what is considered to be the purpose of their teaching.

This, of course, has long been a controversial subject. There are those at one extreme who would urge that the schools concentrate entirely on the 3 R's, limiting their further instruction to the teaching of "essential" knowledge and "useful" skills. At the other extreme are those who would have the schools fit the student solely for intellectual pursuits. In the large sprawling middle ground are those who advocate the fusion of both extremes, maintaining that the primary function of the school in a democracy is to ensure a steady supply of people who are equipped to live—as well as to make a living—in a democracy. If they are to do this, they argue, the schools must teach some facts, of course, but they must also stimulate inquiry into many facts and instruct in the evaluation of all of them. They must teach the fundamental skills; but they must also offer values to govern the use of those skills. They must give instruction in specific fields of knowledge; but they must cultivate respect for all knowledge. They may at times have to teach *what* to think about a given issue; but they must also teach *how* to think about any issue or, in other words, how to think for oneself.

Our concern here is not with the role of the school in a democracy but only how the schools can help to bring about a reduction in prejudice. It is obvious that if these institutions were to accent the utilitarian exclusively, or even heavily (as the prejudiced invariably advocated), they are bound to turn out large numbers of efficient, technically competent young people, respectful of authority, skillful in their chosen trade, and perhaps even enthusiastic about the mechanical wonders of our age. It is difficult to imagine, though, how this assembly-line education could produce men and women of flexible intelligence, appreciative of the human as well as the mechanical possibilities in life, given to wonderment over the infinite complexity and variety of individuals as well as their inventions.

If education is to help importantly in the attack upon prejudice there must be changes in its practice as well as in the principles that govern it. Respect for the individual can hardly be taught in a school that practices segregation, or employs no teachers from minority groups. And even if the schools were permitted to broaden their program so that they might become better training grounds for life in a democracy, we need no extensive investigations to tell us that many teachers presently in the public schools are ill-equipped, either by training or inclination, to carry out such a program.

Many teachers still consider the obedient student to be the best student. Many still are more inclined to punish than to investigate the causes of persistent inattention, misbehavior, and failure to learn. Each time they do so, of course, they greatly increase the possibility that their dull or truculent pupils will become even more rebellious and unreasoning adults. Not many teachers have more than a hazy notion of the relationship between mental health and mental aptitudes, and fewer still have any idea of the connection between prejudice and personality development.

In a recent study of prejudice in the Philadelphia public schools, reported by Trager and Radke in their book *They Learn What They Live,* it is stated that practically none of the teachers was aware of the link between self-acceptance and the acceptance of others. Hardly any was aware of the crutch prejudice so frequently provides for the crippled personality; few realized that the hostile child might be a distressed child and that his anger might be a symptom of his own uneasiness, rather than a response to the untoward behavior of others. Most of the teachers took a benign view of the hostilities revealed by their youngest pupils, describing as "harmless name-calling" the epithets many of their children hurled at one another.

They did not believe prejudice became "a real problem" until early adolescence anyway, and then most of the teachers had their pet remedies for dealing with it. Some believed it sufficient merely to have classes made up of "all kinds"—on the theory that when one mixes with "all kinds," one's understanding is automatically enlarged. Others, equally innocent as to the dynamics of prejudice, took the opposite position, advocating classes composed of "all of one kind" on the theory that by absenting those who "caused the trouble" one avoided the trouble. Almost all seemed to believe that to keep the disturbance from surfacing was to prevent the disturbance from fomenting.

In recent years countless educational leaders and organizations have been working for needed changes in teaching and teacher education. As a result of their efforts heartening changes have begun to be evident. Many teacher training institutions, for example, have begun to modify their curricula to reflect newer insights into child behavior. They are expanding their instruction to incorporate the what and how of *learning* as well as of teaching: they stress not only techniques of instruction but the emotional needs of pupils and the effect of those needs upon the teaching job.

For those teachers now firmly entrenched in their careers, whose training was completed long ago, there are graduate seminars and summer workshops sponsored by colleges and universities the country over. In these, practicing teachers have an opportunity to hear about and discuss newer teaching methods, possible curriculum changes, intergroup education programs, even contemporary social and political problems. Working together on matters of common interest with fellow colleagues and a variety of "experts" of all races, religions, and creeds is in itself an experience that often helps to modify the hostile feelings some harbor toward members of other groups. Each year the number and quality of these workshops grow and each year more and more teachers are attending them, some traveling many miles to do so.

Each year, too, more and more schools, from primary through university level, are incorporating into their basic courses of instruction (in geography, social science, economics, history, etc.) the facts about prejudice and discrimination, their origins and consequences for the victims as well as for everyone else. The problems as well as the contributions of minorities groups are being realistically discussed in more and more classrooms throughout the country. In some communities textbooks have been scanned and, where necessary, retired or overhauled because of hostile or stereotyped references to one or more minority groups.

Activities such as these unquestionably help to reduce prejudice, certainly to discourage the more devastating expressions of it. And although facts can always be forgotten or distorted, in the long run accurate information is a most important ally in the effort to improve human relations.

Community-minded educational groups and education-minded civic groups are hammering home to their members the importance of closer communication between parent and teacher, school and community. For they are increasingly aware that the most enlightened school program can be reduced to a shambles under the steadily hostile gaze of the community. The most stimulating curriculum in the hands of the best trained teacher can bewilder rather than benefit the child if he is unable to reconcile those things he learns at school with his observations and experiences all the hours he is away from school.

In some communities citizen committees, composed of a wide circle of individuals carrying weight in the community, have conducted self-surveys to discover the facts about prejudice and discrimination in their town. In many instances such surveys have proven effective stimuli to action, inasmuch as facts gathered by important citizenry cannot easily be ignored. In some places such surveys have led to city ordinances enforcing fair employment practices, to the employment of Negro school teachers and police officers where none had been employed heretofore, to the admission of Negro doctors and nurses to community-supported hospitals.

Today there are more than five hundred local, state, and national agencies working in some way to achieve a reduction of prejudice. Some of these have this as a primary purpose, others are concerned with it only secondarily. Some of these organizations concentrate heavily upon research, others upon education, and still others upon social action and the securing of legislation to prevent discrimination in employment, housing, and education.

Labor unions, veterans and women's groups, civic and youth organizations are also devoting more time and attention to matters of prejudice and discrimination. Trade unions for some time now, have been conducting intensive educational programs directed to leaders and rank and file members, pointing out the cost to each worker of discrimination within their own ranks. Other civic and special interest groups anxious to promote good citizenship have incorporated into their programs a variety of activities to encourage an appreciation and respect for difference. All these are having a significant effect the country over in providing opportunities for fuller participation of minorities in the social, economic, and political life of the nation.

Working in these ways, both independently and cooperatively, the schools and community groups must come closer to the goal all claim to have: namely, the cultivation of a community of more responsible and responsive human beings. And to the extent that they do, they will be contributing immeasurably to the reduction of prejudice in our time.

But prejudices will flourish in the minds of both young and old as long as their surroundings provoke them and their environment encourages them. In fact, the learning of prejudice is often nothing more than learning "the way things are." Some young children learn to discriminate against others at the same time they learn to dress and to feed themselves. They learn this not by reasoned analysis or because of unreasoning anger, but merely by aping the actions of those around them. Only later do they acquire the prejudices necessary to justify their behavior.

For all of us "the way things are" is the sum and sweeping total of the way most people around us think and act. We are influenced by the opinions of our friends, by the books and papers we read, by the advertising that bombards us, by the programs we see and hear on radio and TV, by the movies and the plays we see or hear about. With all the present means of communication and all the high-pressuring skills employed by these communication centers, to have and to hold a hatred can become as much of an obligation as the use of a particular kind of breakfast food.

Some of us are more easily influenced than others—whether in the realm of ideas or food—by the current fashion. The prejudiced personality is especially sensitive to "the way things are." Even in the prejudices he expresses he governs himself not by what he feels, but by what he believes he is expected to feel. In fact, this may be one reason why we are apt to hear much more prejudice expressed toward Negroes than toward any other group—though there may not necessarily *be* more. For as long as the prevailing view proclaims the indecency of Negro-white relationships, many will feel "safe" and even "correct" in proclaiming the indecency of Negroes.

Similarly, if movies, stories, and plays are weighted down repeatedly with unpleasant characters who are members of minority groups, then the prejudiced cannot help but be encouraged in their prejudices. If avaricious Jews, irresponsible or belligerent Irishmen, gambling Negroes, and Italian gunmen make their appearance often enough, to some they begin to seem like eternal truths. For stereotypes always endear themselves to those who are too lazy to make up their own minds, or whose minds are really no more than echoes of a great many other minds. Just as slogans become graduated into creeds with incredible swiftness by those unwilling or unable to think through their own creeds, stereotypes can become a way of life if they are used often enough. If one sees Negroes cast always in inferior roles, it is easy to believe the Negro *is* inferior—and then to convince oneself that he should be treated so.

Unless stereotypes are regularly and vigorously challenged by the facts, they will not be disowned by those who respect the facts. As long as they are not repudiated by responsible people, they will be used by the irresponsible as proof of "the way things are"; and for some people—particularly for the prejudiced—there is no difference whatsoever between "the way things are" and "the way things ought to be." The fact that some groups have long been persecuted is for him reason enough to perpetuate this persecution. The fact that some groups have always been submerged is for him reason enough to insist that this submergence must continue.

Precisely because neither doubt nor scrutiny are among the tools the prejudiced have learned to use, it is important that we also call into the battle against them the powerful weapon of the law.

"One of the functions of the law," wrote Mr. Justice Holmes to Harold Laski, "is to establish minimum standards of behavior to which men must conform or defy at their own peril. The law works most hardly on those least prepared for it, but that is what it is for. . . ."

The prejudiced personality is constantly on the lookout for clues as to what is "right," "customary," and "proper." Insofar as the law can notify him in the most precise terms of the behavior that is expected of him, it is likely to be a very effective way of communicating with him. Sometimes, in fact, it is the only way because it is the only kind of notice that he will heed.

But the effectiveness of any law depends upon the respect people have for it, and this applies particularly to legislation intended to control the behavior of the highly prejudiced. These must not only be laws that most people want but they must also be advocated and forthrightly supported by the "very best" people. They must be laws that are clear and unrelenting in their purpose and firm in their provisions for enforcement. Above all, they must be applied with vigorous consistency.

This is the lesson to be learned not merely from the *Studies,* but from many years of experience wherever and

whenever people in our country have tried to bring authority
to bear upon one of the most serious consequences of prejudice, namely, discrimination.

Prior to the decision declaring segregation in the public
schools unconstitutional, a wealth of data was brought together for the consideration of members of the United States
Supreme Court. Lawyers, political and social scientists, educators, community leaders, administrators of sundry institutions, all contributed to the record miscellaneous community experiences with desegregation during the last dozen
years or so. These occurred in the armed forces, in schools
and universities, in churches, in places of recreation, and in
public and private facilities of every sort. Some of these
undertakings were the result of state or local legislation,
some had come about through administrative order or town
ordinance, and some were merely attempts to carry out
predominant community sentiment.

Some of these decisions to do away with segregation had
been introduced gradually, others quite suddenly. Some were
undertaken with determination, carried forward with enthusiasm, and administered with confidence. Some were
conceived in anxiety, born in fear, and administered with
an uncertainty that reflected both emotions. Many of these
efforts met with intense opposition; some were impeded
by outbreaks of violence and almost all were threatened with
such outbreaks.

Some of the efforts were quite successful and some were
dismal failures. The successes hardly ever happened overnight. On the other hand, many of the failures came about
because of the decision to impose the order gradually, and
from the outset, therefore, there had been partial and usually

uncertain enforcement. With each day of wavering administration the opposition grew bolder and more brazen until at last it had succeeded in wrecking the entire undertaking.

None of the successes was accomplished without the most careful preparation, which included a variety of efforts designed to create a "climate of acceptance" in the community itself. The preparation, however, also included a realistic appraisal of the strength and the character of the resistance that might be expected.

On the other hand, many of the failures came about because well-intentioned but ill-informed community leaders had insisted that all opposition "must be won over *first*," and accordingly "educational forums" and "discussion programs" were diligently arranged. These, however, were systematically taken over by an opposition incapable of hearing reasoned arguments but exceedingly skillful at presenting and gaining support for irrational ones.

The successful efforts were those that had early reduced to a whisper the voices of their most intense, highly prejudiced opposition. This they did not by the weight of their arguments, but by the number and strength of those who made them. In each instance the most irate opposition retreated not because they realized the possibility of error in their position, but only when they sensed the futility of trying to maintain it in the face of so determined a group. Then, when the hated decree finally became law, those who had initially opposed it were often among the ones most respectful of it—not, of course, of the principles upon which it rested, but of the power and strength behind it.

The influence of legislation prohibiting discrimination on the basis of race, creed, or color is more far-reaching than at first glance it might appear. For it has opened up many opportunities to those who otherwise would have been denied them and without which minorities would have small chance of escaping from their submerged or restricted position. In most of the prejudice expressed toward the Negroes, for example, the belief in their inferiority is pivotal. But with new and unprecedented opportunities, new and unprecedented achievements have been proudly recorded. By their own achievements minorities have provided the most conclusive proof that those "innate" and "inborn" shortcomings of theirs have a remarkable way of disappearing almost (thought not quite) as quickly as the prejudice and discrimination leveled against them also disappears.

As achievements mount so, too, does self-respect; and this is of paramount importance in the reduction of prejudice, for only the self-respecting can command genuine respect from others.

In a contracting economy frustrations expand; when jobs become scarce discrimination soars. Whenever we suffer serious economic setbacks, therefore, we are likely to see and to hear more expressions of prejudice than we might at other times. Doubtless that is why so many people believe that economic considerations are basic in any attempt to treat with prejudice.

As a matter of fact, economic insecurity did seem to be related to prejudice—though not in the way we might expect. For while economic pressures alone do not cause prejudice they frequently unleash it, and unquestionably they aggravate it.

It is important as it is fortunate, therefore, that in our

society provision is being made increasingly to protect people from destitution; to provide a floor below which none can fall and to ensure that no one will be required to go hungry or homeless. It is fortunate too that so many of our country's leaders in all walks of life are beginning to realize that catastrophic economic depressions are preventable and are determined to see that they are prevented. Certainly such measures will make many less forlorn, diminishing the spiritual and emotional demoralization that so often accompanies stark economic deprivation.

But these or comparable measures cannot be expected to reduce significantly the economic anxieties of the prejudiced. For their anxieties flow not from what these individuals lack, but from what they crave—and no matter how much he has, such a person will always crave more. In the healthiest economy, which means an economy of abundance, it is even conceivable that the prejudiced will find more to anger than to relax him. For he is likely to be indifferent to those things he is able to buy and tormented by the number of things he cannot afford. In the realm of the material, the prejudiced is insatiable, although he is no more aware of this fact than he is aware of the reason for it.

The reason is that unconsciously he is yearning not for money or possessions, but for those things that were denied him many years ago: human devotion and the consolation of deep and lasting love. Never having experienced either of these, however, he cannot possibly value them now—but neither can he value anything else. *He is insatiable because he is inconsolable,* and therefore it is not surprising that he should feel angry with the world and a great many people in it—but with himself, perhaps, most of all.

This would seem to suggest that it is our attitude toward money, our economic orientation, much more than our economy, that gets us into trouble. It is true that part of the excitement of America is that anyone can reach for the stars if he feels like it; but it is equally true that part of the problem of America is that so few come within what they consider to be reasonable distance of them. Yet if we were to restrain the ambitious or ridicule the starry-eyed, or impose penalties upon the failures, we might well find ourselves struggling with massive controls and frightening punishments, afflicted by a cure much worse than the disease.

What cannot fail to help, however, is the education of our children and wherever possible, the re-education of adults, so that more people come to know the satisfactions money cannot buy; so that more people learn to measure their incomes in human as well as in dollar terms; so that more people begin to weigh occupational satisfactions as carefully as they are accustomed to weighing occupational status. It might help also if more people were to become acquainted with the facts and the figures concerning America's current economy so that they might adjust their vocational aspirations to them, instead of to the outworn myth of limitless opportunities for those with but energy and determination enough to find them.

"We praise a man who is angry on the right grounds, against the right persons, in the right manner, at the right moment, and for the right length of time." On such a platform we can shake hands with Aristotle. For there are surely reasonable grounds for anger in the spectacle, so commonplace in our time, of those who in their boundless greed are so busy reaching to planets beyond that they cannot take time to open their hearts to the people who live on their own.

But these principles which we would so anxiously espouse through education and protect through legislation are, after all, but extensions of the Golden Rule. They were stated in religious terms long before they ever became political doctrine. Therefore, we might well inquire, should not the religious institutions in our country be pivotal in efforts that so pointedly call for the propagation of their own teachings?

The *Studies'* findings in this area have been substantiated by the observations of countless members of the clergy of all denominations. They draw attention to the potential, as well as to the limitations, of organized religion in the efforts to defeat prejudice—and the limitations have to do not with the beliefs they propagate but only with those who pretend to be believers.

We will recall that the most rabidly prejudiced, the most vehement anti-Semites, for example, were equally vehement about their anti-Christianity. Obviously the church cannot be held responsible for those who so assiduously stay away from it; but neither can it be expected to have great influence with them.

There were, however, a great many who, though not so fanatic in their prejudices, were nonetheless intensely hostile human beings, and a sizeable proportion of these people *did* belong to a church and *did* attend one regularly. These people were churchgoers not for reasons of conviction but of convenience. They went to church not to sustain their faith or even to find faith; but because for one reason or another it seemed advantageous to tag along with those who already had it.

Many religious leaders have expressed their concern over the phenomenon of increasingly crowded churches and increasingly vacant souls. They have asked themselves and one another—and some have sought the help of educators and psychologists—what the church must do and what it has failed to do, to make the true meaning of Christianity known to its worshippers.

Anxious to rectify their errors of commission as well as omission, many religious educators are calling for greater accuracy and truer perspective in the religious education materials, in the teaching of the Crucifixion story, for example, which they now realize could provide the Christian child with profound though unwarranted provocation for enduring hatred of the Jew.

Ministers have decried the practice of segregation based upon color that still persists in many churches. Still other spiritual leaders have called for "something more than the removal of negatives" in religious instruction, urging that the underlying concepts of the Judeo-Christian tradition be more meaningfully taught so that they begin to affect the way people think about themselves and each other not only on Sunday, but on every other day of the week as well.

To the extent that they are able to pursue and to progress toward goals such as these (and a great number are doing so), the churches throughout our land add impressively to the not inconsiderable momentum that already exists in the direction of expanding fellowship, greater justice, and growing harmony among all men.

There are always some who have a ready answer to the problems that arise in a democracy such as ours: do away with some of the democracy. These people must find the

foregoing proposals disappointing and even disquieting
For they are neither sweeping nor dramatic, and there is
nothing even faintly revolutionary about them. Their objec
tive is to strengthen democracy, not to repudiate it, and to
do this by strengthening the myriad social and religious institutions that are its mainstays.

For it is the avowed purpose of these institutions to protect
the individual. It is their function to ensure his security, to
enhance his dignity, and to do this not by submerging his
individuality but by cultivating it. If these institutions are
helped to do their job well, then democracy will function
well. And when democracy works well it can only mean that
more people are finding more reasons to trust than to fear one
another.

9

Know the Difference

> Providence has not created mankind entirely
> independent or entirely free. It is true that
> around every man a fatal circle is drawn be-
> yond which he cannot pass; but within the
> wide verge of that circle he is powerful and
> free. . . .
>
> —ALEXIS DE TOCQUEVILLE,
> in *Democracy In America*

A realistic attack upon prejudice must call forth a thousand
attacks upon it. We must build upon men's faiths but we
cannot disregard their fears. There will be many times
when we might educate, but there will be some times when
we may have to cajole. When we are unable to persuade, we
may have to threaten; and when we cannot influence in any
other way we may even have to punish.

Our success at any one of these times, however, will
depend upon our understanding of the differences between
them. Without such understanding we may find ourselves
trying to educate those who can no longer learn or preaching
to those who at first sound of a sermon automatically become
deaf.

137

As Santayana once insisted that he could not write the life of reason without distinguishing it from the life of madness, we cannot proceed to attack prejudice unless we grasp the difference and the distance between what is feasible and what is not. We would not try to make an idealist out of a confirmed cynic, for example, but neither would we wring our hands in despair over the evil that persisted in his soul. We can decide to control those of his acts that spring from his malevolence in order to keep him from injuring others; but when we have done this we do not rejoice over the reformation that has been wrought within him, for we know that we have only bound him, we have not cleansed him.

We must distinguish too between those efforts intended to inspire and those intended to intimidate—and we must recognize the limitations as well as the possibilities of both. We cannot count upon man's faith in his fellowmen to render him compassionate under all circumstances, because from time to time his faith must be proven justified, otherwise it is blind faith and tantamount to no faith at all. Nor can we depend upon man's fear to hold him in line indefinitely: for fear may cow men and cause them to obey, but sometimes the necessity for obedience creates smouldering anger, and this added to ancient angers can reach explosive force and blow to bits all earlier restraints imposed by fear.

We must perceive the difference between checking the need to hate in the very young and tempering the established prejudices of those already grown; between modifying individual attitudes and modifying the general atmosphere; between changing a person's feelings and changing only his actions. As we are able to gauge the difference and the distance between these, we will become more selective about the battles we take on, more efficient in our preparations for them and more realistic in our expectations concerning them.

If we would keep the young free of the need for prejudice, we cannot forget for a moment the vulnerability of a child and how insistent is his need for love as well as for guidance. And we must distinguish between these two needs, knowing that each is a necessary ingredient of the other, but neither can possibly substitute for the other.

We recall how often the child who was smothered with attention, untouched by discipline, became the adult who searched and yearned for more of the same: a love that would be all-protective and undemanding, to shield him from the travail of maturity. We must remember too that while love alone can not prepare a child adequately for the world he is to live in, guidance unsoftened by love may prepare him to hate it.

The child who is coolly and incessantly disciplined begins early to feel that the world is against him, and when he is grown he may retaliate by pitting himself against all of the rest of the world. Since his earliest guardians had been without compassion and without understanding, demanding but never giving, he will imagine all the other guardians he meets in his lifetime to be of the same disposition. Whether teacher, club leader, boss, army officer, or even the people who govern him, he will respond quixotically to their authority. He may be either too submissive or too rebellious, and often he will leap from one to the other; but whatever the behavior he finally settles into, he will be impelled by fear or by anger, rarely by reason.

The antennae of the youngest are unfailingly sensitive to

the true feelings of those who attend them. The child who loves his parents and who is sure of their love for him will welcome and even seek their guidance. He will not only do as his parents say, but also as they do, and long after he is grown he will continue to model himself after them— adopting their views about life and about people, doing things as they did, taking on some of their habits and even their mannerisms. Furthermore, he will do this knowingly and admit to it cheerfully, as did so many of the unprejudiced adults throughout the *Studies*.

The youngster who senses that his parents do not really love him, or the child who is crushed by his parents' autocratic conduct, may also respect their wishes—and if he has been sufficiently cowed he may even continue to do as they would have wanted him to do long after their demands upon him have ceased. But when obedience springs from fear alone, there is always the possibility that it will end the moment the commands end.

The adult who had been consistently frightened into obedience when he was a child, will often (without necessarily realizing it) set about defying all those ancient orders as soon as he is grown. With his own children he may refuse to administer any discipline whatsoever; and in all his adult relationships he may be equally indulgent. But more often than not his behavior will lack the touch of wisdom, for it was not born out of experience with leniency and it is ignorant, therefore, as to its limitations.

If now this adult is generous in the rights he allows others, it is because no one was ever generous with him; if now he refuses to make demands upon others, it is only because excessive demands were too often made of him. He behaves at the instigation not of benevolence but of resentment; and though this is not always discernible, he acts not out of kindness but out of vengeance.

If, therefore, we would render the young immune from the ravages of hate, we must remember how often guidance that was loveless or love that was guideless in the beginning years created the vacuum that was to be filled in the coming years by deep and unreasoning prejudice.

Nor can we expect teachers to work miracles with the youngsters who are but briefly entrusted to their care. For by the time the youngest kindergartener arrives at the threshold of his first classroom he is in possession of a personality already remarkably well-formed. He may be either sensitive or thick-skinned, dependable or capricious, patient or irritable in the face of delays and difficulties, amenable to reason or inclined to be pig-headed. A child at any age, moreover, may come to school full of joyous anticipation and eager to learn, or brimful of anxiety and much too tense to learn anything at all.

The teacher cannot provide emotional stability; but she should be able to identify emotional distress and suggest to the parent or other appropriate persons how it might be alleviated. She cannot build character or distribute a conscience to those without one; she can, however, encourage some character traits manifested by her pupils and discourage others. She cannot superimpose many new values upon those the child has already learned, but she can extol some and make little of others.

She can also stress the creative rather than the competitive aspects of individualism, and she can stimulate rather than anesthetize her pupils' developing intelligence. She can enrich the learning experience of her bright pupils and minimize the discomfort of the dull ones. And as she is able to help her youngsters to understand the importance of striving, to take pleasure in their own achievements, automatically she helps them to understand how important it is for *everyone* to be able to strive and to achieve. As she encourages them to confront and to surmount their own shortcomings she is encouraging them also to be sympathetic to the shortcomings of others. As she helps them to appreciate their own capacities and to know their own worth she is also teaching them how to gauge rationally, rather than emotionally, the worth and the potentialities of others.

The best trained and the most conscientious teacher, though, can only teach those who are willing and able to learn. The teacher can reach and benefit those who are receptive and responsive to her, but those who are not must become our concern as well.

Because these recalcitrant ones are of school age they are not necessarily the schools' responsibility. Although the teacher should be able to recognize those of her pupils who are too disturbed or distressed to hear her, she cannot be expected to help them fundamentally. Other ways must be found and other assistance must be provided if these youngsters are to be able to profit from their schooling.

If their special needs are not recognized, or if help is not given to them, they will almost certainly become the carriers, if not the foci, of infection for any one of our social ills. These are the youngsters who will busy themselves in crime or try to comfort themselves with narcotics or alcohol. These are also the youngsters who in a few short years may be expected to lead or to swell the morose and militant ranks of the prejudiced.

There has been much talk of the school's responsibility for teaching an understanding and appreciation of the differences that make up America. In fact many schools do provide impressive instruction in the customs, traditions, and miscellaneous religious and national backgrounds of those who live in our country. While such information may add considerably to the pupils' sophistication, it does not necessarily affect their attitudes. A knowledge about differences does not automatically help one to respect those who are different. And sometimes such instruction is so intent upon its message of diversity that it overlooks or underplays the story of our similarities.

As Norman Cousins observed in his book *Who Speaks For Man?* it is important to teach the true facts about differences among us, but to stop there is like clearing the ground without knowing what it is we would build on it. Teaching them about differences must be done in such a way as to help youngsters to appreciate the true significance of the American nationality—which is not in the details of its separate strains but in the aspirations that are common to all of them.

The schools can provide a small part of this instruction, but in its entirety it is a long course. For facts alone cannot endow one with the ability to reflect upon the common ground shared by all of mankind. A storehouse of information is not required to render one capable of speculating about the similarities that underlie and transcend the differences among us. One needs rather the capacity to use a few fundamental facts in such a way as to be able to relate each to the other, rather than to separate one from the other.

In his book *The Measurement of Adult Intelligence*, Dr. David Wechsler describes a "Similarities Test" which he considers to be among the best of the entire battery of adult intelligence tests. In this the individual is required to tell how paired items resemble one another: in what ways for example, a banana and an orange are alike, a coat and a dress, a wagon and a bicycle, an eye and an ear, a poem and a statue. There are twelve such pairs in all and as the list progresses the items seem on the surface to become more and more unlike, although their similarities become more significant.

An infantile mind will perceive no similarity whatsoever between a wagon and a bicycle; a less infantile mind would notice that both have wheels, and a more mature observer will remark that both are means of conveyance. "There is an obvious difference," Dr. Wechsler explains, "both as to the maturity and the level of thinking between the individual who says that a banana and an orange are alike because both have skin and the individual who says that both are fruit. As already noticed by Terman and others, it is not until the individual approaches adult mentality that he is able to discriminate between superficial and essential likenesses. But it is remarkable how large a percentage of adults never get beyond the superficial type of response."

The ability to *relate* rather than to *separate* things as well as people is not something one learns merely by being told that such relationships exist; it is something one must feel because one has experienced similar relationships. This perception is not an adjunct of knowledge, but rather an attribute of maturity: that incalculably subtle mixture of information and experience, sight and insight.

While neither teacher nor parent can present a child with maturity both can become aware of the obstacles so often put in the way of a child as he proceeds toward it. They can provide him with information that will serve to reduce his ignorance, and expose his rationalizations concerning those who are different from himself. They can clear his path so that he travels unhindered in the general direction of maturity. And as they do so they will be reducing his own need to hate and building within him immunity to the prejudices of those around him.

To blunt the edges of prejudices in those who are no longer children, we must distinguish between what is flexible and what is fixed in the attitudes of adults. For while we are all faithful and even fettered to our earliest teachings, few of us remain unaffected by the circumstances of the hour. By adulthood one's character may be constant, but the circumstances surrounding it are not, and it is these that so often determine our actions. While prejudiced adults have a great deal in common no two are alike even with respect to their hatreds; for as these have a variety of origins they have also many different natures. Some prejudices may be of recent origin and relatively mild and conciliatory; others may be more rooted and therefore more tenacious. Some will surface readily and frequently; while others are cautious and show themselves almost reluctantly.

Some individuals assume the prevailing antipathies because they are too timid to disclaim them; others because they are afraid to face up to their real troubles. Some would be happier without their prejudices but others might be miserable were they to be deprived of them. Some of the timid, for example, would shed their prejudices swiftly the moment they observed that almost everyone else was dispensing with theirs. Some of the practical would relinquish their prejudices the moment they were convinced that they had more to gain than to lose by doing so. Some of the intensely hostile may never give up their prejudices, although even they could probably be frightened into silencing them.

Knowing the differences in the origins and the consequences of prejudice, we cannot expect ringing appeals to brotherhood to move those who have nothing but hatred for their brothers. Brotherhood begins with self-hood, and one who is busy deploring himself or fleeing from himself can hardly be expected to hear or to heed his brothers' cries for help.

Nor can we expect pious appeals for justice to arouse those who think only of the injustices they themselves have had to endure. We would not anticipate anything but a shudder from the highly prejudiced when he is entreated to support "equal opportunities for all," for we know now that he feeds on the myth of his own superiority and if he is to have no better opportunities than anyone else, even he dimly suspects that he would be no better than anyone else.

Nor would we appeal to the sympathy of those who have never known sympathy and are therefore likely to be barren of it. For as we urged them to imagine the plight of the weak and the downtrodden, they could only be reminded of their own plight long ago—an image more likely to evoke fury than sympathy.

We would not serenely propose "mixing of all kinds" or "free association" as an unqualified cure for prejudice; for we know that while some association and mixing may help to modify attitudes of those who are educable, the hostile and uneducable will use these experiences as they use every other experience, to prove how ill advised is such association and how justified is their own prejudice. Prolonged association, moreover, must be on an "equal status" basis otherwise it will intensify rather than dissipate the stereotype. This happens, for example, when Negroes and whites are in constant and close association but the Negroes are always servants and the whites are always their employers.

The highly prejudiced are prisoners of the moment, to a much greater extent than the rest of us, in that they lack the courage and the independence to express an opinion that is not at the moment in style. At the same time, however, they never truly hear an idea unless it echoes those they already have. When the *Studies* warn that appeals to emotion will often be more effective than appeals to reason, they are saying in effect that it is easy to sell despair to those who are already desperate. But the method has not yet been devised for selling hope to the chronically gloomy—no matter how superb the salesmanship. And this, essentially, is what must be done if we would change the feelings as well as the behavior of the prejudiced.

For the absence of hope is crucial in their personalities. If they could dispense with their pessimism they would doubtless also dispense with many of their prejudices. But in most their pessimism has been too firmly planted in the distant past to be amenable to contemporary reason or up-to-date logic. It may be treatable but only by methods that strike at its root causes: by means of individual psychotherapy or special forms of group therapy. Such treatment, however, is available to only a fragment of the population and even if it were to be available to more, the prejudiced would be the last ones to seek it out and because of their rigidities the least able to benefit from it even should they wish it.

We may not be able to argue the highly prejudiced out of his feelings, but we can control some of his actions that spring from them. For he will modify his behavior, we now know, not out of consideration for others but to spare himself either criticism or punishment. When we use legislation to prevent acts of discrimination, therefore, we must keep clearly in mind the difference between the purpose of such legislation and what we hope may one day be its effect. For the purpose of the law is to control the disorderly, not to reform them.

"If I were having a philosophical talk with a man I was going to have hanged," said Mr. Justice Holmes in the same letter quoted earlier, "I should say, I don't doubt that your act was inevitable for you but to make it more avoidable by others we propose to sacrifice you to the common good. You may regard yourself as a soldier dying for your country if you like. But the law must keep its promises."

In a democracy laws cannot be justified on the grounds that they are for someone's moral or spiritual good; they may turn out to be, but that would be an incidental effect of the law and not its purpose. Its purpose is to protect the many, not to improve the few.

We often hear it said that legislation may increase prejudice even while it reduces discrimination, for it must only make the angry more hostile when they are required to act in a manner so contrary to the way they feel. This may be so. But a democracy has a right to defend itself and the law is one of its weapons. From time to time, therefore, the people in a democracy may decide that it is necessary to anger a few in order to keep faith with the many.

In most places where such laws have been in effect long enough to estimate their influence, all but the most fanatically prejudiced after a while seem to find it too great a strain to maintain two faces: one for themselves and the one they wear for the public. Ultimately then, to save their public faces, they will insist that the way they are acting is the way they want to act, and characteristically they will declare that the way things now are is the way things ought to be. The habit of defending themselves seems ironically to lead them to approve the law by which they now abide and even to forget how ruefully they came by it!

We referred earlier to the cardinal importance of anti-discrimination legislation in promoting the self-esteem of those for whom it serves as an entrance-way to freedom and equality. But even as we recognize the importance of self-respect among members of minority groups in order that they may gain the respect of others, we should not imagine that this in itself will end the prejudice against them. *Prejudice must be cured in the prejudiced, not in their victims,* although there are some things their victims can do to discourage their oppressors and therefore to protect themselves.

If their would-be victims show a promising vitality, for example, the prejudiced can be counted upon to be cautious in dealing with them. For even the most ruthless of wrecking crews will pause in their work when they find that the structure before them is of steel not clay, that it is sturdy and well buttressed, and that its demolishment will require greater skill and fortitude than they had bargained for.

In sophisticated circles it is often argued that if members of minority groups were to improve their manners and demeanor they would see an immediate improvement in the feelings of others toward them. But those who argue in this vein are shutting their eyes to at least half of the facts in their eagerness to believe the other half. Because of this self-induced blindness, they fail to distinguish between cause and effect insofar as the behavior of some members of minority groups are concerned.

As far back as their memories take them, there are some who can recall that the members of their group have always been measured by a yardstick different from that used to measure other groups, and it is to be expected that they might hate the world for requiring this, and themselves for permitting it to happen. In such a situation it is to be expected that some of these people should feel no mood but despair; that they should find no other outlet but to burst forth in arrogance lest they attack—or castigate themselves incessantly lest they weep. Those who would judge their behavior, therefore, if they would judge it justly, must also be willing to judge the circumstances that provoked it.

Behavior of minorities, no matter how offensive, is never the cause of prejudice, though it often stirs up antipathies already there. In every interview for the *Studies,* those low in prejudice would explain unpalatable actions they observed among members of an oppressed group as the *result of* rather than a *reason for* the prejudice against them. The highly prejudiced, on the other hand, were more interested in condemning than in explaining, and unhesitatingly they would spin from the misbehavior of any minority member an elaborate justification for their intense dislike of all of them.

As minorities come to accept themselves, they must come to perceive more clearly the nature of the prejudice expressed against them. They must come to understand that, as they are not the cause of it, neither are they the only casualties resulting from it; that as they ward off attacks upon themselves they are warding off subtle but unmistakable attacks upon other of their countrymen. In their own efforts, then, they cannot but be heartened by the realization that they have many allies from among the "majority" groups in America—people who because they respect themselves and their country find it impossible to accept serenely the raw reality of many of their fellow-Americans who are still unjustly shackled.

It is of importance to all Americans that minorities understand and respect themselves. For the American does not spring from one nationality or one tribe or one country, but from all the civilized nations on earth. And the most powerful identification Americans have with one another stems not from the similarity of some of their backgrounds but from the variety represented by all of them, and the comforting assurance that theirs is a country that presumes to attach no greater weight to one than to another.

So profound is this identification, in fact, that it is practically impossible for any American to think ill of himself without thinking ill of others who are in so many ways like himself. If any American is to respect any other American he must begin, therefore, by respecting himself: a pride in, and respect for, one's own heritage becomes a prerequisite for a pride in, and respect for, America itself.

Respect—not tolerance—must be our goal if we would diminish prejudice in our time. For tolerance is often but a gentle disguise for prejudice: the tolerant often behave as self-appointed connoisseurs of weaknesses in others, or self-appointed protectors of those whom they deem to be their inferiors.

Psychologically, there is a strong resemblance between the stridently "tolerant" and the prejudiced. For while the one may descend to attacking whole groups of men and the other may rise to a passionate defense of them, both are equally indiscriminate in their attack or defense; and neither has any concern whatsoever for individual character. To insist that we love all men is not much different from insisting that we hate most of them, and those who insist upon either course are usually covering up some abysmal emotional vacuum in themselves—perhaps an inability to love anyone at all. Intolerance on proper grounds and on the proper occasion is a sign of maturity, and one should possess the ability to hate even if the impulses in that direction are feebler than the impulses to love.

The issue is not who is to tolerate whom, but the grounds on which men should be required to respect one another. The difference is that where there is to be respect there can be no commitment in advance—either to hate or to love: there can only be a commitment to consider each man on the basis of his own merits and his individual qualities. There can be only one promise: to respect all who deserve respect, regardless of race, creed, or color; to denounce all who deserve denunciation, regardless of race, creed, or color; to permit the same opportunities to all who qualify and to insist that the qualifications required be the same for everyone, regardless of race, creed, or color.

To be capable of executing this promise, however, one must be capable of accepting the existence of evil as well as good in all men—and in one's self to begin with. But when men become aware of their imperfections, no matter how aware they may be also of their potentialities, tumult, confusion, and fear is inevitable. The only element that can cut through all these, that can steady and support human beings under such circumstances, is the element of hope. And as it is an essential element in reducing men's fears, so it is also an essential element in reducing their prejudices.

The hope of which we speak is not simply a philosophical concept, it is a vigorous working theory. In fact, history serves far better than philosophy to illustrate the crucial importance of hope in translating men's faiths into reality. It might be said that America was born because of it; but it *must* be said that without it she would never have survived.

In his vivid and penetrating account of the founding of our Constitution, Carl Van Doren tells in *The Great Rehearsal* of the bitter dissension between the proponents or friends of the Constitution and those who were its enemies.

The friends of the Constitution, he relates, hoped and believed that it would contribute to the world "a principle as well as a faith" concerning the inalienable rights of mankind. The enemies could only imagine that it was "the work of crafty men who were conspiring against the people" in order that they might create a government in their own interest.

The friends of the Constitution hoped and believed that it would become a "rule of life to be lived by the people and their children, and their children's children." The enemies of the Constitution believed that its words were mere rhetoric, that its principles could never be preserved because the people lacked the energy and the will to preserve them—and therefore it would make way for the most "iron-handed despotism."

The friends of the Constitution, we are told, rested their arguments on their belief that there was more nobility than degradation in most men; the enemies rested theirs on the certainty that malevolence virtually consumed all men.

More than one hundred and sixty years later, writing with all the advantage of historical perspective, Mr. Van Doren reminds us that the Constitution came into being because those who had hope refused to credit those who did not; and that "those who believed were more right than those who doubted."

Will future historians, looking back upon the disquietude of our own mid-century, be able to say of us that those who lived by their faiths were more right than those who lived by their fears?

Sources

This book is based largely upon the following four volumes:

Anti-Semitism and Emotional Disorder, by Nathan Ackerman and Marie Jahoda.

The Authoritarian Personality, by T. W. Adorno, Else Frenkel-Brunswik, Daniel J. Levinson, and R. Nevitt Sanford.

Dynamics of Prejudice, by Bruno Bettelheim and Morris Janowitz.

Prophets of Deceit, by Leo Lowenthal and Norbert Guterman.

A fifth volume, *Rehearsal for Destruction*, by Paul W. Massing, a study of political anti-Semitism in imperial Germany, though helpful as general background for the author, was not a source for *The Fears Men Live By*, which is a story about America and Americans.

These volumes, comprising the series *Studies in Prejudice*, were edited by Max Horkheimer and Samuel H. Flowerman, and published by Harper & Brothers. The author is greatly indebted to the American Jewish Committee, sponsor of the *Studies*, for permission to use their materials.

Helpful information, insights, and perspectives were gained from the following:

The ABC's of Scapegoating, by Gordon W. Allport (Association Press, 1942).

And Keep Your Powder Dry, by Margaret Mead (William Morrow, 1942).

Escape from Freedom and *Man for Himself*, by Erick Fromm (Farrar & Rinehart, 1941, and Rinehart & Co., 1947).

Faces in the Crowd and *The Lonely Crowd*, by David Riesman (Yale University Press, 1950 and 1952).

Frustration and Aggression, by Dollard, Doob, Miller, Mowrer, and Sears (Yale University Press, 1939).

Group Relations and Group Antagonisms, by R. M. MacIver (Harper & Brothers, 1944).

The Heritage of America, by Commager and Nevins (Little, Brown, 1951).

Main Currents in American Thought, by V. L. Parrington (Harcourt, Brace, 1930).

Personality: A Biosocial Approach to Origins and Structure, by Gardner Murphy (Harper & Brothers, 1947).

Personality: A Psychological Interpretation, by Gordon W. Allport (Henry Holt, 1937).

The Psychology of Social Movements, by Hadley Cantril (John Wiley, 1941).

Psychology and the Social Order, by J. F. Brown (McGraw-Hill, 1936).

Puritanism and Democracy, by Ralph B. Perry (Vanguard, 1944).

Race: Science and Politics, by Ruth Benedict (Modern Age Books, 1940).

Racial and Cultural Minorities, by Simpson and Yinger (Harper & Brothers, 1953).

The Reduction of Intergroup Tensions, by R. M. Williams (Social Science Research Council, 1947).

Resolving Social Conflicts, by Kurt Lewin (Harper & Brothers, 1948).

Social Psychology, by Otto Klineberg (Henry Holt, 1940).

The Social Psychology of Prejudice, by Gerhart Saenger (Harper Brothers, 1953).

Social Theory and Social Structure, by Robert K. Merton (The Free Press, 1949).

A Study of History, by Arnold Toynbee (Oxford University Press, 1947).

They Learn What They Live, by Trager and Radke (Harper & Brothers, 1951).

Commentary magazine was the source of many articles providing information and enlightenment before and during the preparation of this manuscript.

The author also found illuminating *Studies in the Scope and Method of "The Authoritarian Personality,"* edited by Richard Christie and Marie Jahoda (Free Press, 1954), and was glad to have the opportunity to check her own interpretations against those up-to-date evaluations of some of the original *Studies.*

The following sources were particularly helpful in the preparation of the chapters indicated:

CHAPTER 2
BOOKS: *Race Awareness in Young Children,* by Mary Ellen Goodman (Addison Wesley Press, 1953). ARTICLES: "Authoritarianism in the Interviews of Children," by E. Frenkel-Brunswik and J. Havel (*Journal of Genetic Psychology,* 1953, 82); "Generalized Mental Rigidity as a Factor in Ethnocentrism," by M. Rokeach (*Journal of Abnormal and Social Psychology,* 1948, 43); "Some Roots of Prejudice," by Gordon W. Allport and B. M. Kramer (*Journal of Psychology,* 1946, 22).

CHAPTER 4
BOOKS: *The American Dilemma,* by Gunnar Myrdal (Harper & Brothers, 1944); *Caste and Class in a Southern Town,* by John Dollard (Yale University Press, 1937); *Growing Up in the Black Belt,* by Charles S. Johnson (American Council on Education, 1941); *The Mark of Oppression,* by Abraham Kardiner (Norton, 1952); *The Negro in the United States,* by E. F. Frazier (Macmillan, 1949).

CHAPTER 5
BOOKS: *Anti-Semitism,* edited by E. Simmel (International Universities Press, 1946); *Essays on Anti-Semitism,* edited by Koppel S. Pinson (New York Conference on Jewish Relations, 1946); *The Jews, Their History, Culture and Religion,* by Louis Finkelstein (Harper & Brothers, 1949); *The Making of the Modern Jew,*

by Milton Steinberg, rev. ed. (Behrman House, 1952); *A Mask for Privilege,* by Carey McWilliams (Little, Brown, 1948); *Moses and Monotheism,* by Sigmund Freud (Knopf, 1939); "The Psychology of Anti-Semitism," by Israel Wechsler, in *A Neurologist's Point of View* (Wyn, 1950); *Punishment Without Crime,* by S. A. Fineberg (Doubleday, 1949). Articles: "Portrait of the Anti-Semite," by Jean-Paul Sartre (*Partisan Review,* 1946, 13); "The Psychoanalysis of Anti-Semitism," by Otto Fenichel (*American Imago,* 1940).

CHAPTER 6

Books: *The Appeals of Communism,* by Gabriel Almonde (Princeton University Press, 1954); *Heresy, Yes; Conspiracy, No,* by Sidney Hook (John Day, 1953); *The Need to Believe,* by Mortimer Ostow and Ben-Ami Scharfstein (International Universities Press, 1954); *Prescription for Rebellion,* by Robert M. Lindner (Rinehart, 1952); *Report on the American Communist,* by Ernst and Loth (Henry Holt, 1952). Articles: "Political Creed and Character," by Robert Lindner (*Psychoanalysis,* Winter, 1953); "Receptivity to Communism," by Herbert Krugman (*Public Opinion Quarterly,* fall, 1952).

Acknowledgments

It is not possible to acknowledge individually the many friends who influenced this work in some way. There are a few, however, to whom I am particularly indebted.

It is a special pleasure to acknowledge the help of Clifton Fadiman. His belief that this book could and should be done was a major determinant in my decision to attempt it. His counsel at many stages of its writing was invaluable.

I must express my deep appreciation also to Alan Green for his many valuable suggestions, his indispensable editorial advice and guidance, and for his encouragement all during the writing of *The Fears Men Live By.*

I owe a special debt to Irving M. Engel who in many different ways helped to make this volume possible.

I am indebted too, to a number of former colleagues at the American Jewish Committee: notably, Edwin J. Lukas for his critical reading of Chapters 4 and 5 in their early drafts; Milton Himmelfarb and Joseph Gordon for their counsel on Chapter 6; Dessie Kushell Cohen for much general aid and comfort throughout this entire undertaking; David Danzig for several provocative and fruitful lines of thought; Selma Silverstein for cheerfully tracking down and forwarding to me, much pertinent material. I should like especially to acknowledge the help—without involving him in responsibility for the results—of Marc Vosk, of the Department of

Scientific Research, who several times suggested leads for me to follow and criticised constructively both an early and later draft of this manuscript.

My thanks also to Dr. Frank Trager for his critical reading of Part One and Part Two in their early drafts.

I am grateful to Helene F. Margulies who suffered the numerous re-typings of the manuscript before the final version reached the publishers. There, I appreciated particularly the practical suggestions and advice given to me by Ordway Tead and Hermine Popper.

The time and therefore the opportunity to undertake this book was made possible by the generosity of the Lederer Foundation, the Lucius N. Littauer Foundation, and the J. M. Kaplan Fund.

The courage to undertake it initially and to stay with it despite recurrent periods of despair and discouragement came to me through my husband, Dr. Joseph Hirsh. His acute understanding of my task was matched only by the devoted assistance he rendered whenever he was needed, which was constantly. My gratitude to him is greatest of all.

S. H.

Index